FIGHTING THE TALIBAN

FIGHTING THE TALIBAN

THE MEMOIRS OF AN AFGHAN ARMY COMMANDER

BASHIR SAKHAWARZ

Pen & Sword
MILITARY
AN IMPRINT OF PEN & SWORD BOOKS LTD.
YORKSHIRE – PHILADELPHIA

First published in Great Britain in 2024 by
PEN AND SWORD MILITARY
An imprint of
Pen & Sword Books Limited
Yorkshire – Philadelphia

ISBN 978 1 03610 064 3

A CIP catalogue record for this book is available from the British Library.

Typeset in Times New Roman 12/16 by
SJmagic DESIGN SERVICES, India.
Printed and bound in the UK by CPI Group (UK) Ltd.

Pen & Sword Books Limited incorporates the imprints of Atlas, Archaeology, Aviation, Discovery, Family History, Fiction, History, Maritime, Military, Military Classics, Politics, Select, Transport, True Crime, After the Battle, Air World, Frontline Publishing, Leo Cooper, Remember When, Seaforth Publishing, The Praetorian Press, Wharncliffe Local History, Wharncliffe Transport, Wharncliffe True Crime and White Owl.

For a complete list of Pen & Sword titles please contact
PEN & SWORD BOOKS LIMITED
George House, Units 12 & 13, Beevor Street, Off Pontefract Road,
Barnsley, South Yorkshire, S71 1HN, England
E-mail: enquiries@pen-and-sword.co.uk
Website: www.pen-and-sword.co.uk

or

PEN AND SWORD BOOKS
1950 Lawrence Rd, Havertown, PA 19083, USA
E-mail: uspen-and-sword@casematepublishers.com
Website: www.penandswordbooks.com

MIX
Paper | Supporting responsible forestry
FSC® C013604

Contents

This book is dedicated to the Afghan, British and US armies, who fought without fear the evil force of the Taliban.

Chapter 1

Army Barracks, Mazar-e Sharif, Afghanistan, 2013

I had been waiting for the daylight the whole night. It was the longest night of my life. When the call for morning prayers came and it was still dark I could not leave my bed like other days to go for ablutions and then to the mosque. I was exhausted. While I wanted to get out of the army barracks, I had no energy to do so. I heard other officers getting out of bed, preparing themselves for *namaz*. It is embarrassing not to go for prayers unless you are sick. Indeed, I was not physically sick but mentally. Before going for my daily duty, I got up, went for a wash and stood next to the entrance of the barracks.

Last night was much quieter than other nights but still the noise of army helicopters, incoming and outgoing rockets continued. I have become immune to such noises. The noise of bombs and rockets does not bother me. A soldier must have a good sleep because it is the mind that saves a man with a gun, not so much his physical condition. I have also learned to survive without food and water for a long time but keep my mind alert. And yet last night I could not sleep because there was another war within me.

In my right hand I was holding a letter from my wife Jamila, the cause of my sleepless night. I'd read its contents more than ten times, almost as if by reading it over and over again the contents would change. The letter basically said that our baby was breech. The discomfort of pregnancy had forced Jamila to travel from Nijrab district to Kabul with my father for a check-up at a government hospital and she was informed that the baby was breech. She had two options: caesarean birth or the doctor would try to change the position of the baby. Jamila told the doctor that in Nijrab we have a very skilled midwife who has saved many women's lives and she'd be able to help. Jamila is shy and uncomfortable with male doctors. She prefers to be in the comfort of her own home in the hands of Allah and the midwife. Of course, sending her to a private clinic would be the best option, but that would mean spending a huge amount of money. Since the fall of the Taliban, private clinics owned by foreigners have started operating but only rich people can afford to go to them. These clinics are much cheaper than those they went to in the past, in Dubai or other countries. Some even own property in Dubai. As for me, although I get a much better salary than the average Afghan citizen, I cannot afford a private clinic or travel to Dubai.

The earth, the sky, our compound, my feelings were all hot and I was boiling inside my army clothes, holding an American cigarette between my sticky fingers, standing next to Jamshid, who by now had stopped comparing our heat to the heat of Texas. I was mentally between many things. His real name was Joshua but I cannot pronounce it, so I'd given him an Afghani name. Jamshid said he loves his new identity. "In a new language you must have a new name," he said, and I was impressed because I hadn't managed to learn his American name and yet he spoke Farsi just as well as I did. He had been here for seventeen months and had only occasionally been able to visit his wife and son in Texas.

"'In these times personal life is not important, we must think of the lives of the masses.' This is what Pasternak said in *Dr Zhivago*."

"What are you talking about?" I looked into his eyes, thinking he was talking nonsense again. He said many things I didn't understand and, frankly, didn't want to understand because his explanation was just as bad as not explaining.

"Oh, never mind, Amir. Pasternak was a Russian writer who wrote *Dr Zhivago*."

"Bloody Russians," I said looking at the hot sky, flicking my finished cigarette away. He did the same. We had learned to finish our smoke at exactly the same time and we liked each other very much because of our similar circumstances. We were both far from our wives and we were both at war. Since I joined the army I had rarely been to Nijrab district where my family lived. Now Jamila was expecting her first child and there was bad news in her letter.

"Commander Safi says that you cannot go home now to see your wife?" Jamshid asked.

"You are correct."

"You see, Pasternak was right."

"Leave the effing Russian alone." I smiled. "You are here to tell me how to get Hazrati Sultan district back."

Hazrati Sultan was only two hours' drive from Mazar-e Sharif where our army compound was, one of the strongest compounds in the country and yet the Taliban were brave enough to attack it, forcing the district administrator to flee. Of course, this was a publicity stunt. The Taliban could have attacked a more remote place and held it longer.

What happened in Hazrati Sultan was a typical act of dishonour and distrust on the Taliban's part. Just a month before, they had met with General Safi in an unofficial capacity, verbally agreeing that they would not attack areas under Safi's control, and that was a great concession because General Safi was in charge of the Northern Zone. The whole country was divided militarily into four zones: north, south, east and west. That showed how important General Safi was and he was allowed by the Afghan government to negotiate unofficially. So he gave assurances to the president, not aware that the Taliban wanted to discredit him by attacking a district just two hours' drive away. He'd taken out our personnel from Hazrati Sultan after the Taliban's assurance, leaving the district an easy target. The general was embarrassed and felt he'd been naïve and now it was time for retaliation, not only by getting Hazrati Sultan back but by targeting some remote districts that were under the Taliban's control.

General Safi was not an ordinary general. He was a rare two-star general who had studied abroad. He was a very tolerant and peaceful man and hoped the war would be over soon. He preferred to talk peace with the Taliban rather than fight them.

Our fortune in war had changed. Now the Taliban were able to attack districts, but our morale had not weakened. We knew that with the help of our allies, the British and American armies, we were capable of taking those districts again and attacking Taliban strongholds, pushing them back. The Taliban had their own international supporters, mainly rich Arab fundamentalists and countries such as Iran and Pakistan, and we suspected that other countries were also involved, otherwise how was it possible that they had almost the same type of weapons as we had, excluding planes and armoured vehicles? They could see us at night using instruments that detect body heat. The Pakistani government, so-called friend of the US, denied it was supporting the Taliban. But even the US knew that was a lie, because the Taliban base was in Pakistan and they got their sophisticated weapons through that country. Iran, the archenemy of the US, did not deny its support of the Taliban and seemed to enjoy being considered a troublemaker by the US. As for Pakistan, it is against a strong Afghanistan because of a long-standing territory dispute that goes back to the formation of Pakistan.

"What is in your hand?" Jamshid asked.

"Leave it, Jamshid. It is not from Shakespeare."

"Stuff Shakespeare, man."

"You are a curious soldier."

"What else can you be in this mysterious land?" he asked, taking a step towards me. "Please tell me."

"Here it is. You can read it."

I gave him the letter and looked around me. The barracks, the army vehicles, the dry land, the hot sun and he next to me, were all the same. All reminded me that I must be with Jamila. He read the letter and then looked at me.

"It's a tough one, bro."

"You're damned right."

"Would you come with me to the chapel?"

"What for?"

"To pray with me," he said with a smile. "I can't tell you what to do. If you go to your wife, you dodge your responsibility as a soldier. And if you go to capture Hazrati Sultan district, you escape your responsibility as a husband. So, what I can offer you at the moment is a simple prayer and you know all answers are in prayers."

He walked towards the chapel and I followed. Sometimes I went to the chapel with him, and sometimes he came to the mosque with me. We both knew that there is one god only and he is not in the category of Islam or Christianity. One god for all human beings.

It was cool inside the chapel, as it was built inside another building, providing extra protection from the heat. Our compound was in the middle of a desert, too hot in the summer and too cold in the winter. Another reason for visiting the chapel was to escape the extreme temperatures. The chapel was empty apart from Jamshid and me. Neither of us uttered a word. In silence, he extended his arm, first putting his hand on my shoulder and then holding my hand as a sign of brotherhood. He'd learned that Afghan men held hands to show affection. We both kneeled and I closed my eyes, imagining Jamshid had done the same. In the darkness I saw images of Jamila in pain and images of innocent people attacked by the Taliban needing help. I was torn between two decisions. If I left my duty as a soldier, I would have failed my people. And if I ignored Jamila, I would have failed my responsibility as a husband. Tears sprung to my eyes, but I fought them back. Jamshid pressed my hand and then got up to leave. I heard his movement without looking at him. I don't know how long I stayed there but it was for a while after he left. When I came, out a patch of cloud had circled the hot sun and the day seemed cooler. Jamshid offered me another American cigarette and, while he held the lighter for me, he said, "There is an answer for you in that patch of cloud."

"You should be a philosopher instead of a killing machine, my friend," I said.

"The cloud says that I must help you."

"You're kidding. But how?"

"We have a helicopter which is used for dispatch and leaves here every morning at 5 a.m. You'll be on it."

"I think the hot days in this country have melted your brain."

"I'll talk to your commander and ask him to give you permission for one day's leave to see your wife and the midwife, so that you feel confident that she'll be okay. But make sure you take the same helicopter in the afternoon of the following day. Please be at Bagram Airport at least an hour before the flight, and don't miss it because I'll lose face. That way you will be almost in two places at the same time. You'll see your wife and you'll come back for your duty immediately the following day."

This time I could not stop my tears. They were tears of happiness and gratitude. While my own people were ready to kill me, this foreign soldier was ready to risk being punished for giving me the chance to see Jamila. What if I did not come back the following day? Of course, I would not have failed him. *Mardara qaul ast*, men do not break their promise.

The day after I was ready by 4 a.m., all dressed in civilian clothes and my beard was long enough to pretend that I was a peasant from Nijrab. My accent in Farsi had never changed despite my education. But I could also easily use words common among the farmers of my district to disguise my identity in case I encountered the Taliban. The helicopter journey to Bagram Airport was about thirty minutes. As soon as I landed I took a taxi to my relative's house in Kabul. From there I took another taxi to Sarai Shamali, from where I had to get yet another long-distance taxi, or a bus that operated between Kabul and Nijrab, about 80km away.

When I reached Sarai Shamali, instead of taking the bus, which would have taken longer, I jumped into a taxi departing from the same place and asked the driver to drive fast, hoping to get every single minute I could with Jamila. The young driver was kind and he did not even stop for a break. When we reached Solanak, the top of a hill notorious for Taliban ambushes, from behind a rock two Taliban jumped on the road pointing Kalashnikovs at the driver. The young man just managed to stop the car half a metre from those guys and I smelled the burning of tyres on the road through the open windows. Without any words, the Taliban pointed to us with their weapons and ordered us to get out of the car. While one of them kept the gun aimed at us, the other searched the car, almost destroying the seats, taking everything out of the boot, even looking underneath the chassis, while we both kept quiet, fearing if we said anything they would shoot us. It was a remote place and no other car was passing. After an extensive search, the one who was searching came to me first.

"Show me your papers," he said.

"What papers?" I asked using my Nijrabi accent but also words familiar to peasants.

"Your ID, you idiot."

"I don't have any," I said, opening my jacket wide for them to search. He searched me.

"Everyone was given ID by the government a year ago."

"I am an illiterate peasant and while the government was distributing IDs I was on the mountains cutting wood for fuel."

"For the whole month?"

"Yes. I was coming down and going back. I had a contract."

The man went to the driver. "Don't tell me you are a peasant too."

"No, sir. I am a school graduate and here is my ID and driving licence."

The man looked at the documents with care, matching the driver's face to the document. After a while he asked the driver, "Why did you not join the army instead of doing this? The pay is much better."

"I don't want to, sir. And besides, I have an old mother to look after."

"We'll look after your old mother," the man who was pointing the Kalashnikov said, laughing. Then he spat his snuff on the ground and shouted, "Let them go."

I was aware that Taliban might appear from anywhere so I had left all my ID and documents in Kabul with my relative. If they'd found a single hint that I was an army officer, they would have killed me on the spot.

After a three-hour drive, I was finally sitting next to Jamila, who was having an afternoon nap. I told the others not to disturb her and just listened to her breathing, watching her chest expand and contract until she opened her eyes.

"Amir, is it you?" she said with a surprised smile.

Chapter 2

Mujahideen

I was just 7 years old when the Mujahideen came to power. My father said if the UN and other countries around the world did not put pressure on our president, Dr Najib, to sign a peace agreement and transfer the power to the Mujahideen, the Mujahideen would never have managed to take the country, even without the support of the Soviet Union, because by now Afghanistan had trained army officers and soldiers. Despite the soldiers pulling out of the country, there was a regular supply of arms from the Soviets and economic support continued. Pulling out of Afghanistan was great for the Soviet Union economy because there was no big army in Afghanistan to support logistically, and there were no casualties either. The Kremlin was happily surprised and regretted not withdrawing sooner, leaving the Afghan Army responsible for defending the country. The defence of the country was a matter of life and death for the Afghan Army because they knew that as soon as they were defeated the Mujahideen would slaughter them and their families.

For many years my father was an army officer fighting the Mujahideen. When he started to live a civilian life and became an ordinary farmer, my mother and I were very happy because now he was safe and would spend time with us. But not all of us seemed to be overjoyed. Amin, our labourer, who worked in the fields during my father's absence, was worried that my father would tell him his service was not required because Father would fill his position. But one day, when the two men were eating potato stew with tandoori Bolani, my father looked at Amin and said, "You know, Amin, why these potatoes are so delicious?" Amin stopped eating, smiled and thought for a while but could not find an answer. "They are delicious because there are honesty and love in them and you are the reason for that." I could see surprise in Amin's eyes.

"In that case it must be you who have been working, Masjidi," Amin said.

My father returned the same kind smile and said, "No brother. I just collected them with you. But you made them grow like this while I was absent. I thank you for all your effort looking after my land and family when I was away."

The once serene face of Amin now bore the weight of concern, etched in furrowed brows and a slightly agape mouth. He must have thought my father was going to tell him he wasn't needed any longer and, because he was an honest man, he could not stop himself from asking the crucial and dreadful question. "Does this mean you don't need me anymore? Because you have returned and, frankly, you can do the job of two men?"

I put the palms of my hands over my ears, worried that my father would say yes. I loved Amin just like I loved my father, because he looked after me like a father. Sometimes he took me to his house and his wife, despite their poverty, prepared delicious food for me. Going to his house also gave me an opportunity to play with Anwar, his son, who was my age.

I was so relieved when my father said, "No, my friend. Contrary to what you think, you will be needed much more than before. I am thinking of many projects and I fear that even two of us will not be enough, especially in autumn when we go to the mountains."

"Mountains?" I said, nearly jumping off the *dastarkhan* cloth on which the food was laid. "Can I come with you?"

"We go in autumn and it can be cold, besides it is a long journey."

"Please, Father."

Knowing how much I loved him and hearing such good news, Amin found the courage to say, "Colonel sahib, we can take warm clothes with us for Amir and he could ride the mule both ways, as he is so light."

The comment made my father laugh and I could see that in his heart he appreciated the love Amin had for me.

The name Masjidi means someone who is religious and attached to the mosque but my father was neither of those. He was an honest communist who also believed in god. For such a man it was impossible to make an honest and poor man redundant.

My father watched political events closely, seeing if the retaliation against the army had started. His plan was to take us to Iran where he had some contacts. As a young man he'd spent some years in Iran working in a factory owned by a rich man. That was before Khomeini. The pay for Afghan workers was very good but since the Soviet Union invasion, many Afghans became refugees in Iran, making the work environment hard because of the competition to find a job. Now, after the collapse of Shah, and the taking over of the country by the Akhunds, the Iranian economy was bad, especially after the war with Iraq. My father was not even sure if the factory was still working and if the rich man was still in Iran, but he was hopeful that if the worst came to the worst he would be able to take us there and find a job. He told us, however, that it would not be an ideal situation for him because when he went before, he was young and Iran was a rich country. The money he'd earned there was now invested in Nijrab buying more land. We had a good-sized plot and we could even sell our produce in Kabul. My father worried about his house and land in Nijrab, thinking if he went, it would all be confiscated by the Mujahideen, while their main aim would be to kill my father.

Retaliation against the Afghan Army never happened because as soon as the Mujahideen took Kabul, they started turning their guns against each other. The centre of fighting shifted from the countryside to the big cities where the power was. There were not just two or three Mujahideen groups fighting each other, but ten of them. One god divided by ten versions of Islam. One street in Kabul was owned by one group and another by another group, making it difficult for the residents to move around, unable to take their sick and injured to the hospital. My father continued to go to Kabul to sell our produce there and told us horrible stories of how the Mujahideen had razed the city to the ground. Kart-e Char, where our relatives lived, was flattened now but, fortunately, our relatives had fled the country even before the Mujahideen arrived. My father said the war also continued along ethnic lines. The Hazara group hammered nails into the heads of captured civilian Pashtuns and the Pashtun fighters raped and cut off the breasts of the Hazara women, cooking them for their husbands to eat. Barbarianism had no limit and those who thought the Mujahideen would settle their differences soon, because they were defenders of Islam and united against the Soviets, were wrong. The fighting intensified day by day. While the rest of the country was bombarded and unsafe, Nijrab was now in absolute peace and we could not hear the sound of guns or army helicopters.

Shoes were my biggest problem. When I was only 6 years old I injured my hips in a *lingak* competition. It was entirely my own fault for being too competitive, picking a boy four years older and much heavier. *Lingak* is a team game holding one leg, hopping with another towards the opposite team, challenging one and wrestling, trying to make your opponent fall or stand with both legs. If that happens the opponent loses.

The team leaders always loved to have me on their side because I could finish one boy quickly and then go to the assistance of my teammate. To impress my leader further, I challenged a big boy who made my other teammates run away. I managed to pick him up and throw him on the ground but at the same time I felt a sharp pain in my hips. I had to sit down and could hardly walk home. My father thought the pain would go away but he was wrong. After a week of painful walking, my father took me to a specialist in Kabul. After some examinations and X-rays, the specialist said that there was no medicine that would help me but that my father should take me to an excellent shoemaker the specialist knew and to whom he had sent his other patients before.

My injury happened at the beginning of the Mujahideen rule when Kabul was safe. So taking me to the specialist and the shoemaker was not a problem. But now, after two years of wearing the same shoes, I needed a new pair and Kabul was no longer safe because the Mujahideen were fighting each other. The shoes had really helped with my pain, and I really needed a new pair. My father tried to find out when there would be a truce. Once there was, we could go to Kabul.

We got on the bus in the middle of the night, knowing that other people from Nijrab would have heard about the truce and would also be going to Kabul in the morning. Way before dawn even the roof of the bus was full of passengers.

My father continued going to Kabul three times a year to sell his produce directly in the capital, eliminating the cost of a third party, but when he heard that one of his friends from the army had been detained in Kabul and disappeared, he thought it was wise to send Amin instead. Amin was an honest man and my father trusted him.

It is true that the Mujahideen did not go from door to door to find army officers who worked for the communist government in the past, but if they were seen on the street and were recognised, they disappeared. So my father could have sent me to the shoemaker with Amin, but I was his son and he wanted to take care of me. I was delighted to see Kabul with my father. He'd taken me before the war and I liked the city.

We reached Kabul without any trouble but when we came to where the shoemaker shop was we were shocked to see the whole shop was rubble. For a while my father and I stood in front of the place where the shop had been until my father asked the tailor next door, Jawad, whose shop was undamaged, what had happened to Safdar's shop. Jawad told us he was Safdar's brother and the shop had taken a direct rocket hit. Luckily it had been during the night when the shop was shut. Now the poor man was working from home at Kart-e Sakhi.

Happy that Safdar was alive, my father could not hide his worries after we left Jawad's shop, telling me Kart-e Sakhi was only inhabited by Hazaras and they did not welcome other ethnic groups since the civil war had started. Our faces were easily recognisable as Tajiks and Commander Masoud, who was also a Tajik, was the arch-enemy of

Mazari, the leader of the Hazara groups. But we had no alternative. Safdar was now working from home and his home was in Kart-e Sakhi.

When we reached Kart-e Sakhi, we noticed men looking at us but nothing happened. Some even pointed us towards the Takia Khana where the Hazaras went to mourn the killing of Hossain, the grandson of Prophet Mohammad. Safdar's house was in front of the Takia Khana. We are Sunnis while the Hazaras belonged to the Shia sect of Islam. We also mourn the killing of Hossain, but not as strongly as the Shias, who beat their chests with their hands and their backs with metal chains. I had not seen it but my father had told us that he'd seen hands and backs covered in blood. Since we do not mourn the loss of Hossain this way, some uneducated Hazaras think the Sunnis were behind the killing. The ridiculous thing is, it happened 1,400 years ago and who cares what happened that long ago?

We had almost reached the Takia Khana when three young Hazara men approached us.

"Are you looking for Takia Khana?" the older of them, wearing a grey turban and white *piraan wa tonbaan*, asked. He had a beard but it wasn't long and his face was tanned because of the sun. All three of them carried Kalashnikovs.

"Yes," my father replied.

"Why?"

"Because it is in front of Safdar's house, who makes shoes for my son."

"You could not find any Tajik shoemaker that you have to come here?"

"Well, yes, but you see, the doctor advised…"

"You are lying and you plan to put a bomb in Takia Khana to destroy it."

"But we do not carry any bomb."

"Maybe not now. This time you are here to do your research." My father took my hand and pulled me towards him to walk away.

"Where are you going?" the man shouted.

"I have no time, I must see Safdar and take a bus back to Nijrab."

"No, you are not going anywhere, you come with us." The man pointed the gun at my father.

"Listen, my good man, I am not the person you think I am and besides that I am with my son."

"Your son, doctor, Safdar are all good cover-ups but you won't fool me; come before I shoot." My father looked at the man and then looked at me, seeing the fear in my eyes.

"Don't worry, son, there is a misunderstanding; we'll do as the man says."

We followed the three men and now all those people who had looked at us indifferently at the beginning were looking at us as if we were criminals and were really there to blow up the Takia Khana. These men did not know that my father had been to a different Takia Khana before the civil war and had showed sympathy.

We passed an alleyway that was dark even in the middle of the day. The place had a foul smell and there was sewage running down the middle. Rubbish was strewn everywhere, and stray dogs searched for food. The smell and the sights made me think of the wildly different smell of wild flowers in Nijrab and the unlimited green fields with the mountains in the distance. How could children grow healthy in this place, I wondered.

My father's assurance gave me hope that we would be released after some investigations. These men were probably taking us to their leader and the leader would be wise enough to let us go.

We entered a two-storey house with a big courtyard in the middle. The first floor was surrounded by balconies. *Asha daar* windows carved by skilled carpenters pronounced the beauty of the house, but now plaster was falling off the walls, and the wooden balconies creaked underfoot – there were plenty of men on the balconies, in the rooms and on the courtyard.

"Look who I found?" the leader of the three shouted with triumph.

"Who have you found, Murtaza?" one of the men on the balcony shouted back.

"Takia Khana blower."

"Soon we blow his ass in the air," another man from the courtyard shouted and he laughed. I knew at that point that we were in real danger. My father would be killed and I would become a child soldier fighting for them.

"Let's do it now," the man from the balcony cried.

"*Na Tofan Ali*, we must wait for Commander Tofan to interrogate and decide."

"But he is not here."

"We have to wait. He will come back tomorrow from Bamyan."

We were pushed into a dark cellar and I heard a man's weak voice saying, "Please give me some water for the sake of Allah, brother."

"I am not your brother, you son of a *kanchanee*." The man closed the door from behind.

After a while my eyes got used to the darkness. The cellar was used to store wood for the winter. I could see two men next to each other. One had blood on his face and he was moaning.

"I just wanted water," he said.

"Be patient, my brother," my father said, and he went to sit next to him. I followed.

"They beat us every day, these godless people."

I looked at the other man. He was either unconscious or dead and his lifeless body scared me.

"Is he alive?" my father asked.

"Yes, but I am sure he would prefer to be dead."

After some time, which felt like an eternity, the door of the cellar opened and a man brought us some bread and water. The cellar was very warm and the need for water was much greater. So I only drank water. The man with the blood on his face drank every drop of his water, but did not eat his bread. My father ate a little. We all slept on the floor of the cellar. The unconscious man became conscious before going into a deep sleep again.

We guessed it must have been the afternoon of the following day when the door opened and a man entered asking my father and me to go with him. We were taken to the courtyard. The light in the courtyard blinded me. We were made to stand and it was there I saw four men standing in front of us with their Kalashnikovs on their shoulders. I almost ran away. Were they going to shoot us? No one talked and we were also silent, until we heard someone approaching from behind.

"We found them yesterday, Commandant sahib, near Takia Khana," the same man who caught us told the man who was approaching. As he reached our side, looking at me first and then at my father, he shouted, "Is this you, Masjidi?"

"Oh, Nawrooz long beard, my friend," said my father.

Commander Tofan, whom my father referred to by his first name, rushed to my father and hugged him. I looked at them with surprise, and the other four men did the same.

"Why did you come to Kart-e Sakhi?" Tofan asked.

"I was looking for Safdar the shoemaker."

"Why did you bring this man here?" Tofan asked the man who had caught us.

"Commandant sahib, I thought he was going to blow up our Takia Khana."

"With a small child?"

"You know the enemy uses a lot of tricks. How is it possible that a man comes here to find Safdar, risking his life?"

"Did you talk to Safdar to find out? Go idiot, bring Safdar here. I know this man and I am sure he is not our enemy. I know him better than you know your mother."

In no time Safdar was brought and as soon as he saw my father his face brightened.

"He is my long-time customer, Commandant sahib. His son needs special shoes, advised by a doctor."

"You could not do a simple thing like this yesterday to bring Safdar here?"

"I did not believe him, sir."

He was going to say something more when a slap landed on his face.

"This is how we make enemies, you son of a whore. Do you think by killing this man our problems would be solved? Have you thought that such people have family who would retaliate? If you catch an enemy I understand. But to capture an innocent man from the street who is looking for a shoemaker is only the work of a shit man like you, who I would never leave in charge again when I am not here."

My father wanted to leave Tofan to go with me to Safdar, but Tofan did not allow us. He took us to a nice furnished room and then asked his soldiers to give us breakfast, after which Safdar would be able to measure my feet. My father asked that breakfast should also be provided to the two men in the cellar. Tofan ordered his soldiers to comply with my father's wish, but my father had another request.

"Please exchange those two with another two of your fighters who are captured with your enemy."

"Oh Masjidi, you always think of others more than yourself." He slapped my father's shoulder in a friendly way and laughed. "Anything for you, my friend. I owe you my life."

The breakfast was an elaborate one in a country where war made it almost impossible to have good food, but I didn't have an appetite and yet my father was eating as if nothing had happened. Two days of hunger had given him a good appetite but I wanted to leave.

When we got out of Kart-e Sakhi, I asked, "Father, what was Tofan saying about owing you his life?"

He laughed and said, "Tofan was my soldier. When we were fighting Commander Masoud, I wanted information about his strength and I carried out the mission myself. I got close to the enemy position and asked for two soldiers to volunteer with me. Many said yes but I chose Tofan and Wakil. One Hazara, one Pashtun and myself a Tajik. When we got close to the enemy line, four of Masoud's fighters spotted us and one, who was an excellent sniper, shot Wakil in the head and he immediately died. Now we were two against four. I managed to take two down because I am also a good sniper trained by a Russian elite force. The other two managed to block Tofan's path of escape from both sides. The only way I could save Tofan's life was by showing my head to the enemy. The enemy fired but missed by millimetres, hitting a rock. But that provided a chance for me to kill him. The last one was killed by Tofan. So in fact he is right. I was almost killed saving his life. He noticed blood coming off my scalp. He took the turban from one of the dead men and tightened it around my head. The same day I was sent to the hospital and there at the hospital the doctor said I had shrapnel inside my scalp and if he operated, the danger was I would lose my life. So I have a piece of metal in my head. My soldiers never said no to any mission I gave them because they knew if it was vital, I would risk my own life first."

"But he is now with Hazaras."

"You know, son, war unfortunately provides opportunities for some people. Tofan is an excellent fighter who can use many different weapons. He must be very useful for his leader and earns wealth and respect."

Safdar told us that my shoes would be ready in two weeks and he would leave them with his brother Jawad at his shop. But when my father wanted to come to Kabul to pick them up, my mother did not allow him, saying he was a former senior army officer and many people knew him so instead she suggested he give accurate information to Amin about where Jawad's shop was and send him instead. Amin was a very intelligent man and for him to find Jawad was not a big issue. He went there when there was another truce in Kabul.

After that incident I continued with my daily exercises to improve my feet, whereas before I was lazy. Now I knew that I should not put my life and my father's life in danger by going to Kabul to have shoes made for me. Maybe it was because of the panic that my hips responded and got better. I did not need shoes made by Safdar for me in another two years.

Chapter 3

Father

As a young man, Father went to Iran to see a country much more advanced than Afghanistan. He decided to work there to learn new skills, and he planned to bring those skills back with him, start his own business and participate in building our village. Iran was a university for my father. From the time he spent there working in a factory during the presidency of Daud, he learned many things, including how to produce biogas energy.

One summer day, he gave me a bucket and a spade to collect cow dung to put in a barrel. He then sealed the top of the barrel but fixed a pipe at the top for the gas to get out. He also fixed a tap on this pipe to stop the gas from escaping. After a week or two he connected the pipe to a small gas stove, opened the tap and let the gas into the stove. He lit the stove and, to our surprise, the gas burned. My mother was excited, seeing how this new invention would make the cooking easy for her because cooking with wood was tricky. It always took time to ignite the wood and also created too much smoke.

But my father did not stop by just providing gas for my mother. What he did was an experiment for a much bigger project. He and Amin dug a big hole in the ground in front of our house and they put a strong plastic water container in the hole, filling it with dung, which was my responsibility. He used the same procedure to get clean gas from the cow dung. So, some months after I filled the container, we had gas for the house.

My father's adventurous mind brought many projects into existence and Amin found himself even more occupied. Father bought more cows to produce milk and cheese to sell in the market.

Mother was busy every day milking the cows and making cheese. She also looked after a large number of chickens. The old chicken coop was replaced with a new one that could house about 100 chickens. My task was to collect the eggs. These activities kept us busier than before the Mujahideen arrived, and my mother was surprised to see our financial situation improving.

"You didn't have to join the army when you were such a good project manager, Masjidi," my mother said to him.

Beautiful fresh big and small tomatoes climbed trellises in my mother's garden, making the land colourful. There were also onions, spring onions, garlic, peppermint, and small hot chillies that could burn the throat and the stomach. The garden provided enough vegetables, such as potatoes and beans, to make us self-sufficient. Mother even cut a huge number of tomatoes and dried them on our rooftop for use in winter, but her summer salad, a mix of fresh tomatoes, onions, peppermint and green chillies, all cut to the smallest size, was a mix from heaven. The name for this salad was *shamali salata*, but my father called it *Safia's salata* after my mother, because it tasted very different from others due to my mother choosing ripe juicy tomatoes and using their juice as a sauce.

Father also kept Mother busy at night. Soon she became pregnant and god awarded us with a girl, who my mother named Wida. My father had named me Amir, so this time it was my mother's turn.

Now the schools were closed because of the arrival of the Mujahideen, my father did not allow me to just collect dung and eggs. Every morning after morning prayers, he made me attend the morning lesson in the mosque to learn the Quran.

The mullah seemed to know very little about science, denying that the Apollo 11 ever landed on the moon because the moon was a place where god lived. He also used his wooden stick frequently, beating us without any reason to ensure we feared him. The beating normally happened when a boy, instead of looking at the Quran, gazed elsewhere for a short period. He wanted our eyes to be stitched to the pages of the Quran, reading aloud.

One day, when I was concentrating, making sure I did not take my eyes off the pages, a fly kept sitting on my nose. When I finally waved it away and watched its path, I saw the mullah with his eyes shut, sitting cross-legged with a 5-year-old timid orphan, Hafiz, sitting on his lap. The mullah was bouncing him up and down. I could see what he was doing, but immediately lowered my eyes before he saw me.

I could not concentrate after that and when I came home I was trembling. When my father asked me what had happened I told him the story with tears in my eyes.

The appointment and dismissal of a mullah was a very serious matter and the whole village community got involved with the decision. But when I told my father, he immediately took me with him to the mosque and went directly to the room where the mullah was. He normally slept after the morning prayers but my father, without knocking on the door, burst inside with me behind him, and shook the mullah's shoulder violently. The mullah opened his eyes in a state of shock.

"Tell him what you saw," my father shouted at me. It was hard to give evidence against the mullah because we feared him.

"Tell him what happened, son." This time my father asked me gently and I managed to tell them what happened. The mullah denied it, calling me a liar. When he said that, my father slapped his face while he was still on his bed and then grabbed his beard, pulling him out of the bed.

"I give you one minute to collect your belongings and leave this place," my father said.

In a panic, the mullah put on his *chapan* coat, hurriedly collected what he could see, and ran out. For many days after he disappeared the villagers asked each other where he had gone as he had left some of his belongings behind.

My father did not participate in the village meeting to find another mullah. But when the new mullah was found, he went to him and told him about the plight of the previous mullah, warning him what would happen if he did the same.

But my father was not happy with only learning in the mosque. While he did not participate in choosing the new mullah, he gathered all villagers after the Friday *namaz*, the biggest event of the week, and told them about the need for proper schooling for the children of our village, Jarpiroz. He climbed to the altar, a place for a mullah only, and addressed the people.

"Brothers, the real enemy are not the Mujahideen or the bandits but the lack of education. If we do not educate our children they will be misguided by the Mujahideen and may join them. Or they might believe the bandits' promises of great rewards for committing crimes. They would become our own enemy."

People asked where the children could be taught and who was going to pay for a teacher for them, but my father had already thought about that, suggesting that Anwar could teach the children in the school where he used to teach. When the Mujahideen arrived, they stopped paying teachers and for that reason no teacher was available. By encouraging the villagers to pay for Anwar, he was also helping an unemployed person who had his own family. "Brothers, if we all contribute a little it will not be so much to pay for the future of our children. Surely, we can all afford to pay for the salary of a teacher. It is just the same as we contribute towards the salary of the mullah," my father said.

In 1997 after the Mujahideen were defeated, the Taliban started a war against women. They regarded women as their enemy. In the cities, women were banned from working in offices, factories, schools, and even hospitals. Women doctors were forced to stay at home.

Many women were the breadwinners because they'd lost their husbands in wars and now they had no choice but to sell their bodies to make sure their children did not starve to death. Obviously, the Taliban were the main visitors of these unfortunate women. The Taliban forced young and beautiful women without husbands to get married to them, saying women without *mahram* were unsafe and kindle desires in men to commit sins of the flesh. The streets were empty of women. If a woman was found on the street without a *mahram*, she would be whipped in front of the other citizens, bearing pain and shame. They also introduced their own rules for what women could wear when they were out on the street:

1. A burqa, preferably black, which would cover the woman from head to toe.
2. No white socks because white socks raise desire in men.
3. Shoes should not make a sound because, again, the sound of shoes make men want sex.
4. No nail polish or henna.

At first, when they arrived in Nijrab, the Taliban did not interfere with our way of life, which required women to work in the fields. In fact, women did much more than the men in the fields. There was no doubt that men did the heavy work, such as ploughing. But women fed the family, looked after the gardens, grew all kinds of vegetables, raised chickens, and they spent much more time without a break when they were harvesting.

The first thing the Taliban did was install a mullah as the district officer, and Talib mullahs replaced all mullahs of the villages. My father told us the reason for such a move was to make sure the new mullahs acted like spies, finding out if there was any activity against the Taliban. The Taliban knew that mosques were the centre of all activities and gossip in the villages.

The new mullahs noticed women working in the fields without hijabs, because it was impossible to wear a burqa and work in the field. So they announced their disapproval in the mosques. But the villagers ignored them, thinking surely the Taliban would realise that it was impossible for women to wear a hijab under those circumstances. This caused tension between the mullahs and the villagers, which soon exploded.

One spring day we were all in the field when we heard the sound of gunfire. Since the Taliban had taken over the guns had been silent, so this was a big surprise. Our surprise turned to shock when a villager came running from the district to our village and informed us that the Taliban had brought soldiers from Kabul and they were shooting men and women who were working together in the fields.

My father jumped up, put Wida on his shoulders and shouted at my mother and me to run after him. There was no time to lock the house. My mother kept screaming, asking where we were going and my father was just saying, "Follow me." We ran without a break until we reached Kandi Jan village, located on the top of a hill – a remote place, safe enough from the reach of the Taliban, where a relative of my father's by the name of Dada Ghafar lived.

I had been to Dada Ghafar's house twice during the Eid festivities and knew it would take more than an hour to reach there walking fast. But the way my father made us run, it didn't take nearly as long. My mother, a very fit woman, would have collapsed if we had run any further.

The grim face of Dada Ghafar welcomed us at the gate of the house and we were directed to the guest house. There Ghafar kept asking what was happening and both my mother and I also learned the reason for such an escape.

Ghafar was a tall man with dark skin, thick lips, enormous hands, eyes gorged in their sockets, and he only smiled when he was invited to other people's houses. Kandi Jan, where Ghafar lived, was famous for its remoteness and beauty. Instead of watching Ghafar's face, I kept looking out of the window where I could see a blue sky with cotton clouds sailing in a gentle breeze. The mountains were clear of vegetation but still full of colour from the rocks, which my father told me indicated minerals. One day, before the Mujahideen came, when I was walking with my father after visiting Ghafar and his family, Father gathered some small, deep red stones. He took those stones to Kabul to check if they were rubies but to his disappointment they were not. Nevertheless, those small stones had a colour very close to a ruby in the ring my mother wore occasionally with pride, the most expensive gift my father had given her.

Even during Eid, going to Ghafar's house was not a happy time for me, but it had to be done. My father said he found it hard to pay Ghafar a social visit, so I knew that having to go to his house in these circumstances would be torture for him, as we didn't know when the Taliban would leave our villages and we could go back.

Two souls lived in Dada Ghafar's big body. One emerged when he went to other people's houses and expected the best food. During this time, the darkness on his face became lighter, the lines on his forehead disappeared and he even smiled. But when someone went to his house, even before sipping tea without sweetening, his face became dark, the lines on his forehead deeply ploughed, his lips turned concave and his eyes watched in silence, showing disapproval.

His eldest son, one of the nicest guys I ever met, died in a car accident and for Dada Ghafar to save money on wedding costs, it was natural that his younger son married the dead son's widow. Overnight Rahmat, his second son, became a husband and a father of two young children.

Once, when Dada Ghafar was staying with us, my father and some of his friends, who were also staying, planned a joke. One of Father's friends got up in the middle of the night, woke up the others and went to where Dada Ghafar was sleeping naked, as was his habit. He was in the garden sleeping heavily as he had eaten a lot. Ghafar was also famous for having a large penis. My father knotted a string around Ghafar's penis and tied it to the branch of a tree. When Ghafar woke up in the morning to go to the toilet, he rolled over, catching himself. In terrible pain, he managed to free his penis and then he urinated on every individual's bed in retaliation. My father told that story many times.

One day Father give Ghafar some money – judging by the size of the bundle it was a large amount. Initially Ghafar played the role of not accepting, but he finally did. That money made him happy for a while, but then he went back to normal.

My father did not carry much money, but to make Ghafar happy one night while we were hiding from the Taliban, and without my mother's knowledge, he took a big risk by walking to our house in the middle of the night, using the darkness to hide, to bring back rice, oil and flour to give to Ghafar. I don't know if he went once or twice, because he could not carry a big quantity. Once again Ghafar's mood changed and he became nice. What my father did was very risky, but for him humiliation was worse than losing his life. Fortunately, my father's actions bought us more time and then we heard that the Taliban had gone back to Kabul. Leaving Ghafar with a great quantity of money and food, we headed back to our house one morning before breakfast. I could see how eager my father was to get out of that house.

On our way home we noticed fields destroyed by the Taliban because men had allowed their wives to work in them. On the walls of the houses were written threats, like 'Next time we will burn your houses if you don't listen to us.'

When we reached our farm, my mother wailed at seeing our cornfield completely burned. How could they burn such a green field? I thought. They must have used a considerable amount of petrol. Fortunately, my father had enough savings to buy food from the market in Kabul, because nothing was available in Nijrab. But most of the other farmers left our district, either going to Pakistan or Iran. The Taliban promised security, making sure that the refugees returned to their own countries. But what they did to people made them leave.

Chapter 4

Snow Leopard

When the letter from Uncle Nawab came, my father was very excited. Nawab was not my real uncle and had no blood connection with my family. He was from Kabul, another army commander my father met in the army, and they became good friends. Uncle Nawab had been sent to the USSR to study in an army academy by the communist government and was highly educated as well as being the son of a rich man who had many big gardens in Kabul. His father was a good businessman and knowing that Afghan dry fruit was the best in the world, he exported his garden fruits in large quantities to Europe. My father had been to see Uncle Nawab and his gardens many times, eating good food and drinking Russian vodka. Nawab loved having a good time with his friends, telling my father, "Masjidi! My gardens are the best place to forget the war."

"Well, this is the paradise mentioned in the Quran, the only difference is we don't have to die for it. You have the best apples, grapes, pears, mulberries, and at the middle of your garden is a running stream. And then there are bottles of vodka. The only difference from heaven is that in heaven there are rivers of wine."

Uncle Nawab also came to Nijrab, having lunch and dinner with us under the walnut tree, listening to the sound of *sharshara*, our waterfall, praising the beauty of Nijrab. After the collapse of the communist government, Uncle Nawab disappeared. One day we received a letter from him from California. He had his own small supermarket and he encouraged my father to collaborate with him, sending dry fruits from Nijrab for him to sell in America. His father had passed away and he trusted my father more than his relatives. My father, as a man looking for opportunities, was of course delighted.

In this last letter Uncle Nawab had specifically asked for pine nuts. In the past my father had sent him apricots, raisins and walnuts, all from our garden. But we did not have pine nuts. Pine nuts grew in the high hills of Nijrab, at least a day's journey by foot. To bring pine nuts to our village, one day was required to travel to Ghocholan, one day to collect pine nuts from the villagers, and one day to return. All together, three days and two nights.

I could not sleep well for several nights knowing that my father would take me with him to bring those pine nuts to our village. I could tell my friends that I walked three days to be part of this mission. The journey was only two days, one day to give orders to the villagers in Ghocholan. But a bit of exaggeration is common among children. Apart from being considered a help to my father, I loved our pine nuts, much more than walnuts, pistachios or almonds. It is like the difference between rice and rice. There are many different types of rice but none is as delicious as basmati. Pine nuts were the basmati of all dry fruits for me.

At the same time I was impressed by my father's ability to find opportunity even in a desperate situation like war, when business and work were not easy. My father had the talent of making use of his contacts and since he had always been fair and honest, people trusted him and wanted to do business with him. Export to California was a good example. Uncle Nawab trusted Father to the extent that he sent money back to buy pine nuts, and he also sent money for transportation and other official costs. But then my father also trusted Uncle Nawab that he would share the profit with him.

My father also had leadership qualities, which shone during his army service, and I knew he loved serving the army and his country much more than other things. So I could see a bit of nostalgia in his heart, and the way he dealt with it was to create new opportunities. He rarely talked about these opportunities, choosing to talk about his army life instead. I wish we had the right government and one day

I'd become a soldier like my father. My father was the perfect role model for me and he influenced me very much.

Now that my hips were not troubling me, I was ready to show to my friends that I could do extraordinary things they'd never imagined, and even if they thought about them, they couldn't do them because they did not have Masjidi as their father, the man who pushed limits. In my heart I thought he had the same desire for his son, a limit pusher. My father chose three excellent mules for this journey and he thought of riding the mules first and then letting them walk without a load so that they would not be too tired when they carried the load home. He was always very kind to animals.

It was mid-July when we started our journey. The fields were all covered with green crops, trees full of fruits, and the scent of oleaster in my nostrils together with the smell of chapati bread mixed with the smoke coming from tandoors. It was time for the villagers to have their breakfasts, with freshly baked chapati. But the three of us – Amin, Father and I – had our breakfast very early, because the best time for a long walk was in the morning. By 10 a.m. the weather would be hot and force us to slow our pace. It had the same effect on the mules. Seeing blades of corn in the field reminded me of a time when I was playing hide and seek with my friends, and I saw a young couple, half-naked, kissing each other. I froze in my hiding place, watching the couple and I knew that they were not married or engaged. The cornfields were the playground of young lovers and I wondered if my father had met up with my mother in those fields.

After about three hours riding, my father suggested that we sit under the shade of a tree and let the mules have a rest. In the distance I could see the ice-capped mountains and I could hear the singing of the Nijrab River nearby. When we sat, resting our backs against the tree trunks, Amin started singing:

My mother said your ten fingers were ten lumps of light
You could do anything with them

And she was right
You lightened my heart but alas you burned my soul.

And then to my surprise he took all his clothes off and ran towards the river for a swim. As if this was not enough, my father followed, taking all his clothes off and jumping in the river, shouting, "Come on, Amir, enjoy the summer." So I followed with embarrassment.

After a lunch of beans and rice that my father had carried, we started our journey again until sunset, and then Amin collected some dry branches to make a fire to cook dinner. Father believed in eating well when you work hard and indeed this long journey, which was hilly sometimes, was hard work. He'd carried a chicken he'd slaughtered the day before and Mother had cleaned it, together with some spinach from the farm and other ingredients, such as fresh tomatoes, onions, garlic and potatoes. He made the tea before the fire was used for cooking. The tea tasted excellent and lessened the tiredness, and I knew after a good sleep I would not be tired the following day. After tea, Father made another fire for cooking vegetables. Amin was responsible for cooking the chicken. I watched the two men, the two friends, not employer and employee, busy cooking. Sparks of fire flew to the sky and I watched the sky full of bright stars. The sound of cicadas and frogs filled the quietness because none of us talked about anything. The dinner in that open space was one of the best I ever had and that was a combination of wonderful nature and a tiredness that provided the appetite of a horse. We even ate the bones.

After dinner Amin asked me, "Do you see those seven stars together?" He pointed towards the stars and I focused until I could see them. "You know once upon a time they were seven sisters," he said.

"Really?"

"Do you want to hear the story?"

"Yes please."

"There was a wise king who lived behind Qaaf Mountain. Because he was kind and just, his subjects loved him. But the kind king did not have a son to be his heir. His *wazir* and others high ranking in his government advised him to have another wife to make sure his kingdom was passed to a male successor but the wise king, very much in love with his wife, did not agree. The queen and king tried having a son and, as a result, god had given them seven daughters but no son. The king informed his *wazir* and other high ranking court officials that when he died he wanted all his daughters to rule the country together.

"To rule together had never happened in the past. Brother killed brother to rule the country solely. But now seven girls to rule together was something the people never imagined.

"After the death of the great king, the seven sisters, without getting married, served the nation with kindness, even better than their father. Instead of expanding their territory and causing unnecessary fights, they spent money on infrastructure and helping the poor people, to the extent that no person suffered from poverty.

"But when the enemy invaded, the seven sisters took arms and defended their country even better than army generals because they had all received army training when their father was alive.

"When they were old they chose a successor based on his education and humanistic qualities. Therefore, a young judge instead of a strong army general was chosen on the basis that a wise king would be able to find a good general to defend their country.

"The whole nation prayed for them and when the eldest of the girls died, a bright star appeared in the sky and by the time they all died one after another, seven bright stars appeared in the sky and the people refer to them as Seven Sisters Stars."

By now it was time to sleep. My father had brought two shawls, one for me to sleep on and the other to put on my body. He also folded his waistcoat as a pillow for me. But the two men slept on the grass without anything under or over their bodies. They also made me sleep between them in case there was a snake about.

The following day Amin was talking to me about his trips to Ghocholan when we reached a mountain path full of huge rocks and deep falls. He gave the three mules to my father and came to hold my hand so I would not fall. It was exactly at that moment that my father reached for his gun, stored on the back of the first mule. To my horror a snow leopard with white skin and black spots was watching us from behind a rock, his two eyes focusing on us, ready to jump. We all froze, apart from the mules who started to panic. But Amin reached for their reins and held them so they would not run away. I saw my father aiming at the leopard and the leopard watching him, both frozen. In fact we were all frozen. The standoff continued for a long time without leopard moving or my father shooting, until finally and calmly the leopard walked away and disappeared.

"Masjidi, you could have killed the beast," Amin said with excitement.

"But why?"

"We would have sold its skin in Kabul and made money."

"Not only skin, my friend, but most valuable are its teeth."

"So why not kill it?"

"For two reasons, Amin." My father put his gun on the back of the first mule and tied it with rope. "The first is that you never attack a beast unless it is in self-defence. The second reason is that I cannot kill a beautiful animal and see those amazing eyes close. Of all of us, he needs his skin the most."

Amin knew a man in Ghocholan who could accommodate us and when we reached there the man welcomed us wholeheartedly but apologised that they did not have anything for dinner for us apart from homemade yogurt and cornbread. What I ate that evening was another one of the best dinners in my life, because of my tiredness.

In the morning when I got up, men were already in the living room and my father, with the help of Zamir, Amin's friend, was giving instructions to the pine nut collectors. By the evening three loads of pine nuts, two of a decent size, and one smaller, were ready to be loaded on mules the following morning. When I found out that my father had chosen one small load in case I got tired and needed a ride I protested. But my father said the comfort of his son was more important to him than money. "Maybe one day you will come with Amin instead of me. Thank you for taking the chance to learn from this journey."

When we reached home after three days away, I didn't want to talk about my walk to my friends. Instead I wanted to tell them about the mercy, kindness and generosity of a human being and what I learned from my father. But I knew in my heart that they wanted to see the skin of a leopard.

Father let Amin rest for the next two days, allowing Mother to roast the pine nuts, and then he hired a truck to take the pine nuts and his other produce to Kabul. He had another contact in Kabul, who had the job of packaging and exporting the nuts to California. By exporting pine nuts to California, my father created an income for Zamir, for the villagers in Ghocholan, for the man who packed and sent the nuts to California, and, of course, for himself too.

Chapter 5

Dark Hearts, White Flags, or 9/11

The Taliban closed schools for the girls and this was something Father could not tolerate. After discussing things with my mother and the villagers who were all anti-Taliban, my father decided to teach girls of all levels at our house.

"I'll do my best that they learn what I know," he said to the villagers. He was like a scholar in the Persian language and his maths was not bad either. His main aim was to make sure girls could read and write. Some girls started to love Persian literature and one who, under the influence of my father, could recite Rumi, Hafiz and Saadi from memory, became a poet.

The white mountain turned black because there was no snow anymore. The Nijrab River, which ran on melting snow in the summer, was dry. The drought made life difficult for my father to continue with farming, but he found an English non-governmental organisation official (NGO) who taught him how to grow vegetables that required less water after installing a hand pump close to our house. My father changed his farming style, taking lessons from the British experts, using air, moisture and dew.

"I didn't know how little water we needed for some vegetables," he said one morning when we were having breakfast. He also learned how to keep his cattle and chickens alive. The drought made eggs and milk expensive and because of that my father benefited. While the nation was suffering, the Taliban came up with an amazing idea, and that was to pray for rain. Every Wednesday they collected men from the streets and made them do an extra *namaz* called *istesqa*, which was for the rain. They really believed that they could change the climate just by praying. My father repeatedly told my mother, "If only these idiots respected the west and listened to the Western NGOs working here. One has to respect science." Despite the Wednesday *istesqa namaz*, no rain came and people died because of hunger. The UN now had the task of distributing food to the vulnerable.

The Quran solved everything since the Taliban took over. If you were sick, then you must refer to the Quran or someone who knew the Quran, mainly the mullahs. If you had financial difficulty, the Quran would guide you. If you wanted success, then you must refer to the words in the Quran. If you wanted to defeat your enemy, then you knew what to do. For that reason scientific knowledge was irrelevant because the whole Quran was scientific. Einstein and other great scientists did not have to waste time if they referred to the Quran because whatever they discovered was in the Quran 1,400 years ago. Now schools and universities were closed to girls but boys went without having proper materials or good teachers, because the teachers were either killed or they left the country to save their own lives.

The biggest enemy for the Taliban were women. They brought evil to our country just by being there, making men commit sin, they said. According to the Taliban, the women's voices, clothes, or appearance stimulated sexual desire in men and, therefore, made men commit adultery. And for that reason women must stay at home. House and apartment owners were ordered to paint their windows black so no one from outside could see their women. Women should not go out unless accompanied by a *mahram*, and if they had to go out they must not wear white socks, again a sexual stimulator for men, and must cover themselves under a long burqa. If a woman was caught wearing white socks, she would be flogged in public, and the same rule applied to a woman on the street without a *mahram*. Stoning women to death became common in major cities and we counted ourselves lucky to be in a remote place such as Nijrab.

Each time Father went to Kabul to sell his farming produce, he came back with stories, telling us that Kabul was full of Taliban and Al Qaeda members from Chechnya, Uzbekistan, Tajikistan, Arabic countries, and Pakistan. When the people from the Shomali Plains rose against the Taliban and caused a lot of casualties to Islamic Imaret, the Taliban retaliated and, after killing the men, burned their farms. Their wives were given to foreign Taliban fighters who had come without wives, to support the Afghan Taliban. According to the Taliban, those who fought them were infidels and therefore must be killed and their wives taken as sexual slaves. They supported their argument with verses from the Quran.

Now that the Soviet Union had been defeated, the West lost interest in Afghanistan, letting the people suffer as long as they didn't cause trouble. Even the amount of aid for Afghanistan reduced because the country was considered safe. But the safety of the country came with a heavy price. In many households women were the breadwinners because they'd lost their husbands due to continuous civil war. But now they were not allowed to work. So the number of refugees instead of decreasing, increased by people going to Pakistan or Iran so they could simply be fed. While women were not allowed to leave their houses to work, prostitution secretly increased and the only people who could afford such services were Taliban. In desperation some families sold their daughters to the Taliban for marriage.

The only place that resisted the Taliban was Panjshir. This was due to its experienced war commander Ahmad Shah Masoud and the mountainous terrain with narrow roads that could easily be blocked to stop a Taliban advance. The Taliban attempted to take Panjshir many times, but then they left it alone because it did not comprise a threat. If Panjshir was ignored by the Taliban, Osama bin Laden could not ignore Commander Masoud, for he was a well-known fighter, loved by the Western journalists, especially the French. How is it possible that another Mujahid was more famous than him? And with the money and influence he had he managed to find two members of al-Qaeda prepared to risk their own lives in order to kill Masoud.

Knowing that Masoud loved his popularity in the media, always ready for an interview, two journalists visited the Afghan

Embassy in India and asked to be permitted to meet the ambassador. The ambassador granted an audience to these two journalists from Morocco and was delighted to find out they were adamant about interviewing Masoud. While the Taliban ruled the country, all the embassies apart from Pakistan were the employees of the previous government because no country except Pakistan had recognised the Taliban regime. The Afghan ambassador, who was also called Masoud, knew his boss, Commander Masoud, loved interviews, and he was delighted to enable the journalists to reach Panjshir to meet the commander.

Since they were channelled through Ambassador Masoud, who the commander trusted very much, the journalists were allowed to see Commander Masoud without any checks. They were not journalists at all but they fabricated their qualifications and credentials. Initially one of them asked some questions and then the one posing as a cameraman brought his camera very close to where the commander was sitting. At that point the camera exploded, injuring him and killing the cameraman instantly. The interviewer ran away, but when he was caught he was killed by Commander Masoud's soldiers before there was a chance to question him.

While there was a shortage of food and people died of hunger, the Taliban and al-Qaeda had extraordinary parties. They did not drink alcohol but photos emerged showing Taliban leaders sitting in front of huge platters, cutting the flesh of barbecued sheep with their fat fingers. Their *sofra* had *qabili palau*, different types of vegetables including what was cooked in Pakistan, as they had Pakistani chefs as well as excellent Afghan chefs. There was a variety of soft drinks and desserts too. These people came to power to eliminate corruption and poverty, but they increased them. The difference was that only the Taliban and al-Qaeda could benefit from this system. Anyone else would lose his life if caught. Everything seemed extreme and savage, like when Mullah Omar and bin Laden went fishing using dynamite, killing hundreds of fish by dropping dynamite in the rivers and catching only a small number of fish. When the daughter of

Mullah Omar got married to the son of bin Laden, all senior members of the Taliban were invited and they were treated to lavish food, paid for from the pockets of the ordinary people of Afghanistan. There were also fancy trips to Doha, Dubai, Kuwait and Saudi Arabia when the fundamentalist sheikhs of those countries invited the Taliban and al-Qaeda. To make sure that Taliban and al-Qaeda members of other countries were not left without sex, women whose husbands were killed by the Taliban were forced to marry these people. There was no sense of patriotism or defence of our society's values. In the kingdom of Islam, the way it was interpreted, women and wealth of infidels, those who fought the Taliban, were free to be used by the Taliban.

Masoud's fighters tried to save the life of their leader by putting the injured Masoud in a helicopter and flying him to Dushanbe, the capital of Tajikistan. But some hours after reaching the hospital, he died from his injuries. His death proved his clerics wrong – they had said that Masoud was invincible and could not be killed because Allah himself was protecting him and, to prove it, he'd survived thousands of attempts by the Russians to kill him in the past. Obviously, they knew nothing about the determination of al-Qaeda.

I thought the killing of Masoud would make Father happy because my father fought Masoud's forces while he was an army officer during the communist government. But I was wrong. He told me that at least women could work and girls could go to school under Masoud's control. There was less poverty but now the Taliban were killing our men and selling their wives to Arab al-Qaeda and Arab Taliban. My father, who was also not happy with the communist government, told me the reason he fought for them was to stop a bigger evil, the Mujahideen. And he was right because after the Mujahideen took over, Kabul was destroyed and more than 200,000 people were killed when the Mujahideen started fighting each other.

The Taliban and al-Qaeda celebrated the demise of Masoud. Surely Panjshir would fall in spring the following year. The Taliban preferred to fight in warmer weather, but now it was November, so they had to wait. But bin Laden didn't have time to wait. For him, Panjshir was insignificant and for that reason he plotted 9/11 from his fortress in Tora Bora.

After the fall of the Taliban, it emerged that Bin Laden was living in Tora Bora with his wives and children. Photos show him walking with a cane in his hand or sitting in his library full of books. It was here he met al-Qaeda members from all over the world and where he plotted 9/11, although the whole plan started some years earlier by making sure the al-Qaeda pilots were trained.

The cave of Tora Bora in White Mountain of Afghanistan is big enough for many fighters to take shelter. Just in front of the cave, bin Laden had built his house with the help of masons. The reason for choosing such a place was its safety, because even atomic bombs could not destroy it. Also, it was close to the border of Pakistan, giving him a choice of either hiding or escaping to Pakistan.

In 1996, Khalid Sheikh Mohammed met bin Laden in Tora Bora. There he presented his proposal to bin Laden for an operation that would involve training pilots who would crash planes into buildings in the United States. Al-Qaeda provided the personnel, the money, and the logistical support to execute the operation, and bin Laden wove the attacks on New York and Arlington into a larger strategic framework of attacking the 'far enemy' – the United States – in order to bring about a change to the regime.

Key parts of the 9/11 plot took shape in Hamburg. Four of the pilots and planners in the 'Hamburg cell', who would take operational control of the attacks, including lead hijacker Mohammad Atta, had a chance meeting on a train in Germany in 1999 with an Islamist militant who struck up a conversation with them about fighting *jihad* in the Russian republic of Chechnya. The militant put the Hamburg cell in touch with an al-Qaeda operative living in Germany who explained that it was difficult to get to Chechnya at that time because many travellers were being detained in Georgia. It was recommended they go to Afghanistan instead.

Three of the four plotters who would pilot the hijacked planes on 11 September and one of the key planners, Ramzi Binalshibh, became more radical while living in Hamburg. Some combination of perceived or real discrimination and alienation, as well as homesickness, seems to have turned them all in a more militant direction. Increasingly cutting themselves off from the outside world, they gradually radicalised each other, and eventually the friends decided to wage battle in bin Laden's global *jihad*, setting off for Afghanistan in 1999 in search of al-Qaeda.

Chapter 6

Father Fights the Taliban

We did not have television but Father was a keen listener of the BBC. The events of 9/11 shocked him very much, and he was worried that the Americans would retaliate by dropping bombs on Afghanistan. But he was more shocked when one day a man came with a letter from General Salim, his colleague who had fled to the US. After 9/11, the George W. Bush administration had asked him to go back to Afghanistan to fight the Taliban.

After the formal greeting, which is normal in our society, the general asked my father to pick up his Kalashnikov and join him in Kunduz province, where he was fighting the Taliban successfully.

The Bush administration was advised not to send US soldiers to Afghanistan because the US did not have a base in our country and, logistically, to transport soldiers from another base was costly and time-consuming. The US wanted a quick victory and knowing that there were groups inside Afghanistan who had kept fighting the Taliban since the Taliban took over, the US chose to financially support those groups. Money was obviously a motivation but not for my father. He was determined to defeat the Taliban to make the country safe. When he read the letter he cleaned his gun and no matter how much my mother begged him not to go he did not listen.

The most difficult part of the journey would be reaching Kunduz with his gun because the Taliban had checkpoints everywhere. To walk to Kunduz would take more than ten days. So he contacted the lorry driver who normally transported his goods to Kabul and asked him to drive him all the way to Kunduz, filling the lorry with some useless stuff in huge bundles. Inside one of these bundles he hid his gun.

The task of looking after the family was given to me and Amin. My father made me proud by saying, "You are the man of the family now."

Father hugged the three of us tightly and kissed us on the cheeks. Before he stepped out of the house, my mother said, "What is the point in defending a country when there will be no one living in it. You know that the Taliban will kill us if we fight." My mother did not believe in any war for any cause, including fighting for your own country.

"I will make sure that will not happen. If we don't fight them they will kill us slowly," my father said. After that he turned his face. I saw tears on his cheek but he wanted to hide them. He walked straight towards his destination, not looking back, and I thought that if he looked back one more time, he would return.

Rumours spread that the Americans had arrived in Afghanistan to fight the Taliban, but there was not a single American soldier at that moment in our country. However, we loved the rumours because they created panic among the Taliban. Not many Taliban fighters were posted in Nijrab because the district was not an important place and, if there was any trouble, with just one phone call from the district administrator, Taliban fighters from other places would have arrived within hours. Soon that small number of fighters disappeared, including the young district administrator, who was also an experienced fighter. They all went to either Balkh or Nangarhar, the two hot spots where fighting against the Taliban had started. The leadership in Balkh was in the hands of Dostum but in Nangarhar, Hamid Karzai, who became president of Afghanistan after the fall of the Taliban, was in charge and it was to Nangarhar that my father went. Those who were fighting the Taliban were a mix of experienced and new fighters, but there was not a single foreign fighter among them, let alone Americans, in contrast to the support that the Taliban had from foreign Taliban, including the Pakistanis who would cross the border to assist the Afghan Taliban in no time.

I panicked, and for the first time I turned to religion, joining my mother in prayers. Now, like my father, I was hooked on the BBC, delighted to find out that the Taliban were in retreat. The US were dropping weapons and money for our fighters from the air, but I didn't think that was enough. The Taliban were experienced and they'd defeated many, including the previous Afghan government. Now they had all those weapons that had belonged to the previous administration. I even thought that the BBC was spreading rumours about those fighting the Taliban, showing they were defeating the Taliban to create panic, for a psychological effect.

One evening after dinner I was listening to the BBC when it was announced that the Taliban had been defeated in Balkh and the province was in the hands of Dostum. However, fierce fighting continued in Nangarhar, the stronghold of the Taliban, near the Pakistani border where Pakistani Taliban had come in big numbers to fight.

My mother started working in the fields again after a long time, along with our farmer, because now that my father had gone our farmer was alone. I also helped as much as I could. There was no sign of the Taliban in Nijrab and the news coming from fighting areas was that the Taliban were losing.

Some days later a brave man by the name of Nader Khan stormed the district administration with his sons and sent a message to the elders of our district telling them to take charge and deal with the people until the new government was established. Obviously he believed that the Taliban would be defeated. He, like my father, risked his life should the Taliban return.

Since the Taliban took over, female doctors were not allowed to work and some male doctors left the country, either because they did not like the Taliban or in protest against the Taliban. So *tabibs*, or healers, mushroomed all over the country, saving lives by reciting the Quran. Seeing a great opportunity, a healer from Punjab in Pakistan arrived in Nijrab and our simple-minded peasants flocked to his practice, including women. He could cure everything, he claimed, and people believed him. Soon he became rich, had his own land and house, and was married to a very young and beautiful woman half his age. But now the Taliban had gone, Nader Khan, knowing that the healer was a con man, wanted him to leave too. He gave an ultimatum to the Punjabi healer to leave our district within days, and he said he would ask his Nijrabi wife if she wanted to accompany him to Pakistan or not.

On the day of the healer's departure, his wife was taken into another room and asked if she wanted to leave with her husband. The poor woman was an orphan without relatives and because of that she was worried that she would be left in Nijrab without support. So she also left with the healer. Nader Khan then went to our primary clinic and broke the lock that the Taliban had installed, asking our doctors and nurses to return to work, although no salary could be paid to them just yet. He said the new government would deal with that later. Such was Nader Khan's conviction that he had already started talking about a new government.

There is a proverb in our language about wishing for an evil that brings good. What happened at the US World Trade Center was an evil act, which produced goodness in Afghanistan, making the US fight the Taliban.

The Americans started bombing Tora Bora, the hiding place of the al-Qaeda leader Osama bin Laden, and we knew that when the bombs were dropped, there would be casualties among ordinary people. No bomb hits only its target, especially when it is big. Now the Americans were sending bombers from their base in Uzbekistan. My worry was that one of these bombs might kill my father because Tora Bora was in Nangarhar.

It is a strange world. The Taliban could have continued killing innocents for centuries, stoning women to death, closing schools, cutting off hands, and the Americans would have ignored these atrocities. But now, because bin Laden made a mistake with 9/11, the Bush administration was obliged to retaliate. It was obvious that this war was not to help the Afghan people push the Taliban out of our country but to make fighting against al-Qaeda a vote-winner for President George W. Bush at the next election, to make him a hero who retaliated. We were all aware of Western films. This was a film for the Americans because they attacked from a safe sky but our men were dying on the ground, fighting the Taliban and al-Qaeda.

The news from the BBC was encouraging, telling us that al-Qaeda fighters were moving from the lower region of the mountain to the higher region, and from there were trying to escape to the safety of Pakistan.

The war in Tora Bora, led by Haji Zaman, Haji Zahir and Hazrat Ali, continued for two weeks and resulted in massive casualties. Later on, my father told us that he and General Salim took part in this operation. On 5 December 2001, an Afghan interim government led by Hamid Karzai was created. There was no sign of the Taliban anywhere and on 7 December, my father appeared at the gate of our house, just before sunset.

His hair was grey with dust, his Kalashnikov heavy on his shoulder, his eyes bewildered, but he had a big smile on his face, the smile of victory. He went straight to wash and after that he hugged us for a long time before going to his bedroom to sleep. I did not see him for the next two days. He was eating at odd hours and only once a day, sometimes in the middle of the night. My mother always kept food ready for him. None of us told the villagers about his return because we did not want him to be disturbed. After two days he emerged and went to the mosque to tell everyone that the dark reign of the Taliban was over, because some people still did not believe what the BBC said. Many people came with my father from the mosque to our house to hear what happened to him during the time he was fighting the Taliban and vicious al-Qaeda.

At the beginning, the Americans only watched from a distance to see what the Afghans were doing against the Taliban, knowing that the Taliban had a huge army while the men who were fighting them were outnumbered. What helped these people to fight the Taliban was their motivation, while the Taliban's morale had weakened, thinking soon the US Army would attack our country in full force. Most of them were already preparing to leave for Pakistan, including their leader, the one-eyed Mullah Omar. After the capture of Balkh, the US government become certain that the Taliban could be defeated using the Afghan militia, which would cost much less than a whole US invasion. But when it became certain that bin Laden had stayed in the Tora Bora mountains from where he conducted his operation, including 9/11, the US government sent a small number of elite forces, wearing Afghan dress to blend in with the Afghans. The US ground force was vital for the accuracy of the ground bombing. However, the US presence was not enough to prevent bin Laden's escape to Pakistan. This is the information my father had.

Chapter 7

After the Fall of the Taliban

No matter how much General Salim insisted that my father should continue with his post in the army, he refused. For my father, the enemy was defeated and he had discovered a new life and where he'd also be close to his family. His apples reached Pakistan, his walnuts and pine nuts were delivered to California, his wheat and corn filled the market in Nijrab. He even bought more land and employed more farmers, giving Amin the responsibility of being his manager.

The Taliban had gone until Bush decided to invade Iraq. According to my father, the focus changed from Afghanistan to Iraq because Bush Jr decided to take personal revenge on Sadam because Sadam threatened to kill George Bush Sr. Now it was like a western Hollywood movie and during its production, the Taliban had enough time to regroup. Their first appearance was just like the Mujahideen, another terrorist group. While the Taliban previously condemned the acts of the Mujahideen, because they destroyed roads and bridges, looted and raped, now they were doing exactly the same thing. First they destroyed schools and then they went further by demolishing roads, bridges, dams and even hospitals, killing teachers and doctors and, when journalists reported these atrocities, the journalists were killed too.

When I was 18, I knew it was possible for the Taliban to take some of the remote villages. I wanted to fight the Taliban before it was too late, so I asked my father to allow me to study at the army college in Kabul to become an officer. My father thought that he'd fought for his country and could not stop me doing the same because I wanted to follow his path. But for my mother it was a nightmare. However, being a good wife, she agreed with her husband. Their son would become an army officer.

My father taught me the art of how to use a gun when we went hunting, mainly for deer and ducks. He said I should never use a gun for the wrong purposes and I must be kind even to enemies, and hope I would not have a personal enemy. The worst enemy is ignorance, he said, and people who become enemies of the nation and consequently enemies of themselves are the ignorant, those who are used by Arab fundamentalists to join the Taliban or the Mujahideen, destroying their own country. However, my first training started with him when he taught me how to use different guns, including Kalashnikovs.

For the first time in the history of Nijrab, tourists started coming to our district, thanks to the new tarmac roads and solid bridges cutting the journey from Kabul from eight hours to two. The Ministry of Rural Development was active in all rural areas of Afghanistan, building roads, bridges and irrigation dams, and providing water.

The new road provided a business opportunity for my father. Now he did not have to go to Kabul to get a good price for his apples, mulberries and walnuts because he could get a fair price in Nijrab. The issues of logistics and cost of transportation no longer existed.

But my father went a bit further by contacting one of our relatives who had a grocery shop in California, where the majority of Afghan immigrants lived, and found out they were desperate to receive dry mulberries and walnuts from our country. My father learned the art of packing and obtaining safety certification, and soon he sent his fruit to California, first for a relatively low price. But as demand grew, his prices went up.

For the first time clinics with qualified doctors were established, helping patients get support in Nijrab rather than going all the way to Kabul.

The Ministry of Education built schools for girls and boys all over the district, with books provided by UNICEF. But there was a huge demand for qualified teachers.

The arrival of mobile phones put us in touch with our friends and relatives in all parts of Afghanistan and even abroad. My father joked, "We never had a landline but now with a small pocket phone we can contact President Bush."

It all went well until President Bush invaded Iraq and his focus changed. After the collapse of the Taliban the whole country was safe. We could travel from north to south and from east to west. My father said, "There will be no war anymore. The nation is tired." But both the US and my father were wrong about the determination of the Taliban. They simply moved to the safety of Pakistan, where they received training and became better terrorists, learning how to make sophisticated bombs and how to use modern weapons. Slowly they appeared in remote Pashtu-speaking villages. The Taliban are mainly Pashtuns and gradually they started attacking various districts, even the neighbouring district of Tagab where Pashtuns lived. Their courage worried us. Tagab was only three hours' walk from our home and my father walked to that place many times for business.

It was at this time that I decided to join the army at the age of 23. "We must defend ourselves against the evil of the Taliban," I said when I started completing the form for the army. My father kept quiet but Mother started crying, remembering what happened to my father when he was an army officer.

"Mother, if I don't fight," I told her, "tomorrow the Taliban will take Nijrab, kill men and rape women." I gradually gained my father's support to convince my mother and, eventually, it worked. It worked because he was proud of being a big influence on me.

* * *

As if god was angry with the Taliban, the *istisqa* prayers for the arrival of snow and rain never worked. But now, after they'd gone, our village Jarpiroz was covered by thick snow in the winter. In the morning when we woke up, we saw the footprints of a snow leopard in the field. The beast must have been there at night looking for a sheep or a cow. But the people were vigilant, locking their animals inside. There was continuous rainfall and my father with joy repeated the proverb: "Afghanistan can remain without treasure but not without snow and rain."

In spring the snow on top of the mountains started melting, creating a huge source of water for Nijrab River. The village waterfall became background music for singing birds, fields were covered with green wheat and corn. No space was left. Trees were full of green leaves and blossom. Boys and girls, young and old, ran after each other, and by midday we were all hungry. The scent of baked chapati mixed with the smoke of burned wood made our mouths water, We were capable of eating anything. My father said often, "You know, son, during the fighting, what I missed most of all the food was chapati. I could smell it in my dreams."

Many times I'd seen my father rush home to steal a chapati while my mother was still baking them, then he'd sit in a corner eating it with a glass of water. "Peace brings appetite," he said, and there was peace all over Afghanistan. One could travel anywhere and people who'd been at home for many years because of the war visited other places. The tulip *mela* became famous again, bringing families to Mazar-e Sharif from all parts of Afghanistan to see the whole desert carpeted red with tulips. We all loved life.

Chapter 8

Wedding Preparation

I was the eldest son, so my father wanted to make my wedding the biggest event ever in our village. He told my mother to ask the bride's family what they wanted for their daughter by way of clothes and jewellery. And, on top of that, to show their generosity my parents decided to buy some clothes for my future mother- and father-in-law as well. Using this shopping as an excuse to see another country, my father took my mother and me to Islamabad. We had relatives who had escaped the war and lived in Pakistan now. My father said we could stay with them. One of them was doing well, having opened an Afghan restaurant, which was very popular amongst Pakistanis and foreigners. I think apart from making a grand gesture to buy clothes and jewellery, my father really wanted to see why so many people left Afghanistan to live as refugees in Pakistan. If people from Kabul left, it was understandable, because nowhere in Kabul was safe and some areas were flattened by intensive fighting between different factions of the Mujahideen. And yet there were places like the district of Nijrab that had not been affected by war at all. Since Nijrab was an insignificant part of the country, no one tried to rule it and there were many places like this in our country. My father told me that even if war came to Nijrab, he would never leave. So my wedding provided a chance for him to see the other side and judge by himself which life was better: life in danger or life as a refugee. I think he also wanted to know if he was right to stay in an unsafe country.

We bribed our way to the border of Pakistan and at the border we were surprised to see waves of people crossing on both sides without being checked. There were no border police visible but when we were about to cross, two Pakistani border officers appeared and demanded we show them our documents, which we did not have. One of them demanded my father give them 500 Pakistani Rupees, but my father was not so easily bullied. In the end we crossed the border after bribing them with 200 Pakistani Rupees.

"This is all fun, Amir," my father said after we had crossed.

"You are amazing, wasting so much money bribing the Mujahideen and the Pakistani border police," my mother said.

"It is still much cheaper than paying for visas for three of us. Let's have fun. We are celebrating the wedding of our son by seeing a new country."

At Landi Kutal, a border town in Pakistan, we took a bus to Peshawar City, watching the new country through the windows. The road went up and down, showing us only one type of scenery, rugged mountains. After a while, the journey became repetitive and I fell asleep. I only opened my eyes when my father pulled my arm. The bus was now in the middle of a big crowd and a street seller was selling food and cigarettes. It was just before sunset.

"We have arrived," my father said.

He had already done his homework and knew where to find a cheap hotel. "Namak Mandai, salt market," my father shouted to the rickshaw driver to make sure he could hear him, as the place was very noisy.

"We are going to a salt market?"

"This is the old name of the place. There is no salt there anymore but we can find a cheap hotel."

To make sure we didn't get lost, we all got into the same rickshaw, even though there was really only room for two people. However, as we were hard-working farmers, we were very slim. I was impressed, sitting in a rickshaw for the first time in my life, watching the skilled driver avoiding lorries by what seemed to be only a centimetre. It was thrilling and scary. The other thing I noticed was the wave of people on vehicles and walking *en masse*, and I wondered where they were heading. In my country at that time of the day, things slowed down. But here there was no sign of slowing down. Roads were filled with moving rickshaws, cars, buses, lorries, carts, cows, goats. No space was left between buildings. They all seemed to be on top of each other, proof that the population of Peshawar was greater than the whole of Afghanistan.

The rickshaw-driver stopped in front of a pink-coloured concrete hotel and told us it was a cheap yet good hotel. My father paid and we got two rooms: one for me and the other for my parents.

The Khyber Hotel was a four-storey building with a courtyard at the centre, surrounded by rooms that were connected by balconies, from which we could see guests coming in or going out and the chai delivery people who ran from one side to the other to serve tea and collect used cups. It was less like a hotel and more like a busy street, with shouting from the tea bearers, coughing, spitting and loud music, which we could not understand. This was my first introduction to a foreign country, but my father had already been to Iran and had told me that Tehran was a much cleaner and cultured place. No spitting in the corridors. What we loved about Peshawar was the taste of *chai*. We do not have sweet tea mixed with milk. The sweetness of the tea took my tiredness away. We stayed in this place for only one night. The following day we went to Nasir Bagh where one of our relatives had lived for more than ten years. After a night there we would proceed to Islamabad, where our rich relative lived.

At night I thought less of Peshawar and more of my future wife with happiness and hope. The Taliban brought cruel security in my country. There was no fighting anymore and there was no theft. But if a man stole a loaf of bread because his family was hungry, the Taliban cut off his hand. Now, because of the cruel persecution, if a bag of money was left in the middle of the street, not one person would pick it up. But the peace suited us while we condemned the cruelty of the way it was sustained. My father was now doing even better in his farming and that was why he took us to Pakistan shopping for the wedding. I loved whatever my father did for us. He never thought of saving but cared for his family and tried to keep us happy.

My grandfather died when my father was only 6 years old. Because of that, he did not go to university but finished his secondary education with top grades. My grandmother wanted him to continue but my father felt guilty seeing his mother in charge of the farm while he'd be in Kabul studying. During his primary and secondary schooling, he managed to help at the farm but after he joined the army he was far away from Nijrab district, leaving his mother to deal with the farm. Because of his sheer talent he managed to rise to the rank of colonel and he learned some local languages, including Pashto. For that reason he had no difficulty negotiating with drivers in Peshawar, communicating with locals, or ordering food where Pashto was the language. In fact, he sounded like the locals because he'd already asked people about Peshawar when he was in Afghanistan. When the Taliban took the country, some Afghan refugees returned from Peshawar and they were a source of information for him.

The following day we left our hotel and my father negotiated the fare for a two-person rickshaw for the three of us. It took about forty-five minutes to reach a two-bedroomed apartment in a block. My father was shocked to see Nabi with his three children in that small space, but Nabi seemed delighted to see us.

"You brought the scent of our country to me, Masjidi," Nabi said, while his wife went to the kitchen to prepare the tea for us.

"Well, your country misses you too."

"But I can't return."

"Why? The Taliban have brought complete peace to the country," my mother said.

"I heard about that but I have nothing to return to. Whatever money I had I spent here. I sold our land in Nijrab. You know that."

"But you couldn't have spent all that money on the rent for this apartment."

"No, all my money has been stolen from me."

"Stolen?"

"Yes, Masjidi. A smuggler cheated me, promising to take us to the US. He took all the money I had and I thought giving him that money did not matter because soon we would be in the US. But as soon as he took my money he disappeared."

"The biggest crime is the crime when someone steals from hopeless people. I know how vulnerable refugees are," my father said.

"How did the children cope?" my mother asked.

"Children are incredible. They adapt to a new environment fast. It is like you, Masjidi, when you lost your father, the biggest tragedy in your life. You were only 6. But our people were very kind. I am two years older than you and my mother told me to let you win when we were wrestling."

"Come on, Nabi, I was stronger than you anyway," my father said, laughing.

"Do you want to try now?" Nabi challenged. My father jumped up from his seat, rolled up his trousers and said, "Come on then."

We all laughed.

"It has been such a long time since I have laughed, Masjidi," Nabi said with sadness. "The only thing I have done for my three children is that they all go to a school supported by an English NGO. They are very young as you know. I married very late."

"It is because you refused all those girls your mother proposed and waited for a child to grow up to become your wife, Nabi." We all laughed again. The tea came and the pleasure of meeting our relatives made the tea without any sweetness taste better.

That night, Nabi kept asking about Nijrab, nostalgia in his voice, and my father patiently talked about our village, the people who had got married, those who had died, and those who'd had more children. Then my father asked about refugee life in Peshawar. Nabi said he was lucky that he still had some money to pay for the rent and he received rations from the United Nations High Commissioner for Refugees (UNHCR). However, the Pakistanis distributed the rations and they treated Afghan refugees badly. They also stole half of what was provided for the Afghans. He said the following day he would take us to the refugee camp to get his rations and we could see for ourselves the harsh treatment.

Dinner was a simple kachaloo curry, but it tasted excellent in the company of our relatives. My father and Nabi talked, regardless of how late it was. First the children left the living room and then even I could not keep my eyes open. It was at that moment that Nabi realised it was late and asked his wife to prepare one of the bedrooms for us, which meant disturbing the children, bringing them to the living room to sleep so we could have their room. But my father refused, regardless of how much Nabi insisted.

Their two-bedroomed flat with a tiny kitchen was designed for refugees who could not complain. The dark grey, unpainted plaster walls made the rooms dark, and there was a constant noise from the traffic outside as the apartment was adjacent to a busy road. But I had already grown used to this. My father told our host to prepare our rolling beds in the living room. Soon I was fast asleep – I am blessed by deep sleep. It was still dark and seemed as though it was the middle of the night when the sound of Allhu Akbar, the call for morning prayers, blasted through the loudspeakers. Was the loudspeaker installed in our room? As I jumped off the bed, I saw my father and mother also sitting on their beds. The Pakistani mullahs were very aggressive, making sure no one slept after 4 a.m. I knew these people could go back to sleep after *Fajr namaz*, but the locals had to continue with their business. Strict religion robbed poor people of sleep too.

After a simple breakfast of bread with tea we headed to the Naser Bagh Refugee Camp with Nabi to collect his weekly ration. Crowds of people were lined up in front of a locked food store waiting for a senior Pakistani officer to open it. It was getting warm because Peshawar is a hot place even in the morning. But the officer deliberately tormented the refugees. When his Jeep arrived, all the refugees cheered. Now without queuing they all pushed and pulled and even hit each other to get closer to the store.

Women, children and old men were vulnerable but hungry refugees did not care about that. My father saw a boy of about 8 fall and almost get trampled, but Father rushed to him, pushing others away to reach the boy. He picked the boy up and made sure he was fine and then came back to join us. My father is a very strong man. To our surprise, after about an hour of distributing rations, the police closed the store, claiming the rationing was finished. When the refugees started protesting, the police beat them with their thick wooden sticks. I saw one old man with blood on his face. My father was shocked and asked, "What is happening now, Nabi? They cannot let people die of hunger."

"No, the refugees get their rations in a different way."

"A different way?"

"Yes, by bribing and prostitution."

"What are you talking about?"

"I will pick up my rations tomorrow after bribing the Pakistani officials. Those women who lost their husbands in the war will have to sell their bodies to the Pakistani officials to get their rations."

"But these rations are provided by the UN."

"You tell them," Nabi laughed sadly.

I thought about that boy and the old man. Did they have the means to bribe the Pakistani officials for the food they were already entitled to? My mind was busy thinking about this issue while we sat on the bus to Islamabad where a well-to-do relative of ours lived. During the journey I ignored the scenery. The tragedy had taken away all the joy.

Not going to university made my father turn our house into a library. He had all sorts of books, especially history books, and he encouraged me to read. I must say I did not spend time with books but listened to my father, who told me what he'd learned from books. I thought I had in him a man who could tell me everything available in books.

On our way to Islamabad my father mentioned that he was shocked by the way people were different from us and yet 100 years ago Peshawar was part of our country. What really made him sad was the way Pakistani officials took advantage of vulnerable people.

When the driver overtook other vehicles, avoiding head-on collisions by inches, I realised time and money were more important here than life. My father noticed my pre-occupation and asked me, "Do you know the meaning of the advertisements on the wall of those houses?"

"No, but I see they have the same message. Urdu and Farsi has the same alphabet."

"I am glad you noticed the repetition."

"What does it mean?

"Those adverts offer to cure men's erectile dysfunction and I hope you never suffer from it." He laughed.

"No, he is your son and would never have that problem." My mother joined the joke and we all laughed, although I was embarrassed.

At the bus stop, proper black and yellow taxis waited for passengers. There was no sign of any rickshaws. This bus stop was orderly, not like the one in Peshawar. Father hailed a taxi and gave directions to the driver. I sat at the front next to the driver while my parents sat in the back. The warm wind caressed my hair and now I felt happy, forgetting about the refugee camp. Islamabad seemed a very modern city with boulevards, road islands planted with flowers, tree-lined roads. There were no shops on the side of the roads and no carts, donkeys or pedestrians. The houses were mainly two-storey buildings made out of concrete and painted in different colours. In the distance I could see the mountains and sometimes the taxi passed a green spot where there were no houses. In Peshawar there was no space for greenery. The taxi stopped in front of a restaurant in Section Nine, in a part of Islamabad called Bharestan, after a volume of poetry by our great Persian poet Jami.

As we passed the entrance, a young Afghan man greeted us and guided us to sit, but my father asked for Jabar, the owner of the restaurant who was our relative. The young man said that Mr Jabar was away and would be back soon. My father decided that in order to pass time it was a good idea to have green tea. I don't know how much time passed. I watched the customers and waiters in the posh restaurant, noticing a teenage boy who was a bit clumsy being bullied by the others. Knowing stories of my father when he was just an orphan at the age of 6, mistreated by other boys, made me feel sorry for this boy and I am sure my father felt the same. Obviously, Jabar did not care about this kind of behaviour as long as the restaurant ran smoothly and he was probably proud of himself providing a job for such a teenager in a country where jobs were almost impossible for Afghan refugees. I was thinking about this when a man in expensive Punjabi dress rushed towards us. My father jumped up from his seat and kissed the man's cheeks over and over again, hugging him tight. This must be Jabar, I thought. I was not wrong. He gave me a hug and then greeted my mother. We all sat together and started to talk about Nijrab.

"Your brother has built a palace for you in Nijrab with the money you sent," my father said, smiling at him.

"I hope I see it before I die."

"Don't die, brother, before we have our late lunch."

"Oh no. Forgive me, I was overwhelmed by seeing you."

He got off his seat and headed towards the kitchen. In no time food enough for a village arrived: *kofteh*, *borani badenjan*, *aashak*, *mantoo*, *qabili palau*, *sabzi*, lamb and chicken kabab, a variety of salads and some Pakistani dishes too that I did not know the name of. The food was delicious and I ate until I realised that if I had one bite more, my stomach would burst.

Jabar showed what a successful immigrant he was, but I did not care. I simply enjoyed the food. To me my father was the most successful and respectful of all. He never mistreated people who worked for him and even took the risk of keeping our farmer employed while there was a chance that he would not do well.

After dinner we were served *shir yakh* and *kulfi*, two different ice creams: one from Afghanistan and the other from Pakistan, both made using a traditional handmade method, not using a machine.

After dinner, with Jabar at the steering wheel, me next to him, my father and mother in the back, we were in his brand new Japanese Hyundai heading towards his house. My father admired his new car, but Jabar said he was not satisfied with it and was going to buy a bigger family car, maybe a Vauxhall Sedan. "Yes, bigger for smuggling," my father joked.

"You know you cannot be successful here without smuggling," Jabar said. I was shocked to realise my father's joke was true. We ended up in F-6, which is one of the best places to live in Islamabad, home to many rich people, offering a life of luxury with its well-planned environment.

As soon as the car neared Jabar's house, a security man rushed to slide open the long iron gate. The car entered and the man immediately opened the car doors for us. The late afternoon soft sun shone upon a pedicured lawn, decorated with colourful flowers on four sides. An impressive light-blue two-storey building stood in front of the lawn with overlooking balconies and terraces. The man ran to open the main door for the house and we entered a long corridor that ended in a huge living room furnished with modern furniture. *How did Jabar manage to reach such a level?* I wondered.

Jabar shouted for Anisa, his wife, Naqib, his son, and Nafisa, his daughter, the youngest of the family. When they came, Anisa gave me a long hug, kissing my eyes, showering me with kind words, hugging and kissing my mother. I was amazed by the sight of Nafisa. She was only 2 years old when they left Afghanistan, and obviously she could not remember me. I asked about Zaman, my childhood friend, but was told that he was in his café, another family-owned business. As a child Zaman and I were very close, playing *lingak*, swimming naked in Nijrab River, climbing trees, stealing fruit from the gardens of villagers. Each time I went to their house, Anisa made sure I ate before I left and sometimes she filled my pockets with walnuts and raisins. She was the kindest woman I have ever known. And then from behind the family, a shy Pakistani woman in a green Punjabi dress appeared. "This is Golnar, my new wife," Jabar said.

"New wife?" my father asked in surprise.

"Well, not completely new. We got married about two years ago and I have a daughter who we named Sanam. She's probably asleep."

"I see," my father said, watching Golnar coming towards us.

"Is Sanam asleep?" Jabar asked.

Golnar answered "Yes," in perfect Farsi. She must be very intelligent to have learned Farsi in two years and I guessed that she was probably only five years older than me and at least twenty years younger than Jabar.

Just past nine that night, Zaman, my friend, arrived. We just shook hands, as we did not have the confidence of the elders to hug, because we were both shy. But I could see that we were still deeply connected with our hearts. At that moment, my mother and Anisa left the room for a private chat. They were good friends too.

After the women left, Jabar talked about his achievements in Pakistan and it turned out that most of his wealth came from the *lapis lazuli* and emeralds of Panjshir where Commander Masoud was fighting the Taliban. Now there was no foreign country to support Masoud. Afghan internal affairs were left to themselves to be solved. The west had an objective to defeat the Soviet Union and the Soviet Union has been defeated. Who cared if the Afghans killed themselves? So Masoud sent precious stones to Jabar for him to sell to smugglers in Pakistan to be shipped abroad and, of course, he kept a generous share for himself. For my father there was no difference between the Taliban and Masoud the Mujahideen leader. When Masoud was the defence minister for the Mujahideen's government, he and his rival flattened fifty percent of Kabul, resulting in killing of 200,000 innocent civilians.

"Tomorrow you are not going to the café, Zaman," Jabar said.

"Why?" Zaman asked.

"Because I want you to accompany us to Mauri with your friend Amir."

"I am delighted," Zaman said, winking at me. I winked back.

We were given two separate spacious bedrooms, one for me and one for my parents. I slept very well and in the morning, after an elaborate breakfast, we headed towards Mauri in two different cars, one driven by Jabar and the other by Zaman. My parents and I shared Zaman's car. Zaman told us about the beauty of Mauri, a station for the British Army during colonisation where the British acclimatised before being sent to hotter parts of the country. Pakistan indeed was a very hot country and I loved the idea of going to Mauri.

After checking into a very scenic hotel called Pride of Mauri, we were divided into three groups: my father and Jabar, my mother with Anisa and Golnar, and me with Zaman. I felt this was the best arrangement because I wanted to talk with Zaman to find out about his café and his life, because we shared everything when we were young and I hoped we would do the same now. I wanted to tell him about Nijrab and my engagement.

We left the hotel and I sat next to him in his Toyota Corolla. He gave me a headache by driving too fast, not allowing me to ask a single question. Most of the time I kept my eyes closed because the mountainous road was winding and sometimes it was not to possible to see the oncoming traffic. When I thought it was a beautiful part of the country I asked him to stop the car so we could go for a walk, mainly to avoid his continuous crazy driving. During our walk, we passed an army training centre and a convent school.

"They haven't got rid of the old British system," I said.

"They are shameless, still slaves of the British," Zaman responded.

"You know, after what we have been going through in Afghanistan, I wish we hadn't fought the British, but let them rule so we could get the benefit of their administration system, building dams, schools, universities, hospitals, roads, railways, factories."

"Oh no, don't tell me you want the British." I realised Zaman's resentment and therefore did not pursue the topic.

"You know the reason we are here is to do some shopping for my marriage."

"Marriage to your cousin?"

"No, idiot, to a woman I love."

"Lucky you. It seems that I cannot get married."

"Are you serious? You have a rich father who could pay a dowry even for a princess."

"That is the problem, Amir. My father controls everything. You know we have this stupid custom of matching a girl to a boy from the time when they are babies. After I was born, my Uncle Unis had a girl called Taranom. My father requested that we become engaged, back then. I cannot run away from that."

"How awful."

"It's madness. I'm in love with a Pakistani girl called Shabnam and she loves me too. But when I mentioned her to my father, he threatened to disown me because I would bring disgrace to him and his brother Unis."

I looked into his eyes and realised he was fighting tears.

"Shabnam just got engaged to someone about a month ago but before that she asked me to elope. How can I do that with a father like this?"

We sat on the edge of a road facing the snow-covered mountains, listening to the chirpings of the birds, watching big *neem* and banian trees in silence. What could we say if there was no solution? He took a packet of cigarettes out of his pocket and I had one, my first, thinking I was a free bird like those flying between branches. Money could not give you freedom and could bring you misery. After a long silence we got up and went to a restaurant for lunch. After that I talked to Zaman about Afghanistan and told him that we were lucky living in Nijrab, which was not damaged by war. I told him that when I went to see Kabul, I saw some good parts of the city that had been flattened. Now the Taliban ruled over the ruins of Kabul like vultures. I also realised that Zaman hated religion and primitive customs. In our hearts we remained the same, sharing the same values. But I wished I could help him.

Zaman treated me to lunch and I enjoyed the spicy Pakistani food – a variety of meat and vegetables. After the food we had Kashmiri tea and smoked hookah. My friend was very generous and kind, not allowing me to pay for anything. We stayed for a long time after lunch, drinking different types of tea and smoking. After lunch we went for a walk. The beauty of Mauri was breathtaking. Valley after valley was woven into one another, hills covered with trees, mountaintops white with ice, the sound of water in streams, the chirping of birds. All of this took the image of a war-torn Afghanistan away. We did not talk about marriage and war anymore but joked and laughed as if these moments were our last. When we came back to our hotel, we found everyone on the balcony, on the table a variety of snacks. When we sat down, Jabar left us and came back with Black Label whisky.

"How can you get foreign whisky here?" my father asked.

"I brought this with me – a gift from a British friend who works for the British Embassy."

Jabar poured whisky into two glasses, one for himself and one for my father.

"Pour whisky in one more glass for Amir," my father requested.

"He drinks?" Jabar asked.

"No, but let him have his first drink. After all, this is the time for him to celebrate his wedding."

"In that case, I'll pour one for Zaman too."

Zaman looked at me and we both smiled. The impact of alcohol for the first time in my life was immediate and I started giggling and saying silly things. But Zaman was as solid as a rock, which showed he'd been drinking for a long time.

Two days after returning to Islamabad, my father went with me to Sadar, the best shopping area, to buy clothes. My mother, accompanied by Golnar and Anisa, went to the Mina Bazaar, where only women were allowed to shop for ladies' clothes and jewellery. My father made some excuses so Jabar could not come with us. He did not want to be influenced by his taste, just respecting what I wanted, and he made me go from shop to shop trying on shirwani silk suits until I was exhausted. He bought two suits for me and two for himself and in addition some good quality fabrics. I thought perhaps he wanted to have dresses tailor-made in Nijrab.

In the evening my mother showed us five dresses, three for the bride, one for herself, and surprised us by saying she had bought one for Nabi's wife. My father admired all of what my mother had bought and after showing her the suits that he'd bought, my mother asked, "Two suits for you?"

"No, my dear I also have a surprise for you. I had not forgotten Nabi. One suit is for Nabi and in addition I bought some good quality fabrics for his children. We don't know their sizes."

I was impressed by the generosity of my parents. Of course, Jabar was also generous, but his money came easily while my parents worked hard for every coin.

My father enjoyed being with his old friend, talking and drinking for many days. Finally we said goodbye to our wonderful hosts and headed back to Peshawar to give the dresses and fabrics to Nabi's family.

Chapter 9

My Wedding

I agreed with my father that the main trouble in our country was not the Taliban, nor the Mujahideen, but the lack of education. There was young Zaman, forced to get married to someone he did not love and the woman he was going to marry probably did not love him. She was in Nijrab while Zaman lived in Pakistan. It was quite possible she had also met someone else and fallen in love, but she wasn't allowed to marry that person either. Zaman even asked his mother to talk to his father, to ask if he could be allowed to marry the girl from Pakistan. But Jabar did not agree. His mother was also unhappy and the girl from Pakistan was about to marry someone she did not love. At least four people, if not more, were unhappy because of a marriage that was supposed to bring joy. But in my situation, joy started from the moment I told my parents who I wanted to marry.

Marriages could be tragic, and that was the case with my cousin Asifa. Asifa lost her father when she was a child. Her mother, struggling to feed her children, agreed to marry her to Salah Khan, who offered a good dowry. The trouble was that Salah Khan was already married and much older than my cousin. The reason for his second marriage was that his first wife could not bear children. No matter how much Asifa cried to stop the wedding, it still went ahead. The saddest thing was that after five years of marriage, Asifa did not have a child.

The Taliban had banned music in big cities but Nijrab was isolated, without proper roads, and it took at least six hours to reach from Kabul. To make everyone happy, my father paid for two different music group: one, Haji Hamahang, which I liked, and the other one,

Haji Saifo, to please the villagers. There were no invitation cards sent out because that never happened in Nijrab, but guests could come from any corner, including neighbours and acquaintances. People were simply informed by word of mouth.

Knowing that the village cook was not the best, my father brought in a professional cook from Kabul who was one of his soldiers when he was an army officer. The wedding would be held at the centre of the village for male guests and women were invited inside our house. My father emptied the living room and two bedrooms, furnishing them for the guests.

After sunset, men came to our house with guns, planning to go to the square to shoot into the sky, following our tradition. My father politely refused this kind of celebration and offered them tea and sweets. The reason for such refusal was our bad experience during Asifa's wedding when a teenager not experienced with a gun accidently shot a villager. Fortunately, the injury was not serious. However, it could have been fatal. To surprise the men, my father introduced them to a band of five drummers who marched slowly to the square first and from there to the house of my fiancée. The noise was so loud that people could hear the drums from far away. The drummers once served in the army but were now without jobs because of the arrival of the Taliban. They produced enough noise to make up for the lost time. By the time we came back to the square after walking with the drummers, those who were in charge of lighting the square had kerosene and gas lumps hanging from ropes and tree branches. The darkness outside the square showed how bright the square was. The whole square was furnished with handmade dark red carpets, and there were cushions at the edges for the guests to use. There were all different types of sweets laid out, which would be served with hot tea once the guests arrived. There were also hookahs everywhere for those who fancied smoking.

I was wearing my green *shirwani* hand-embroidered dress that we had bought in Sadar Bazaar in Islamabad and on my shoulders was a Kashmiri shawl. I was very elegant. No one had ever seen such dress in our district. My father had his own cream-coloured *shirwani* with a Kashmiri shawl over his shoulders. We entered the square hand in hand and then he requested the company of some elders to come with us to the house of my fiancée for the *Nikah* ceremony, in which the mullah recites verses from the Quran and asks my fiancée and I if we want to get married.

My mother-in-law was kind enough to take me to where my fiancée waited. When I saw her in that white dress, smiling, her dazzling beauty almost knocked me down. Both shy, we exchanged a few words and then her mother covered her face with a thin chador to present her in front of the mullah and the elders. After the Quran recital, we both made our vows and we were officially married. She rode a horse to our house to be with the women and my father and I returned to the square. I rode another horse decorated with flowers. Soon Haji Saifo arrived and created a storm with his band. Haji Saifo was also known to bring female dancers. Some of these dancers also slept with men for money, but my father had told Haji Saifo not to bring the female dancers. Instead he had male dancers. These young men were shy at first, but they became so excited they could not leave the dance floor. My father pulled me to the centre of the floor and made me dance. At that moment I wished I had Zaman next to me to celebrate my happiness. After the dance my father took me away from the crowd and we went to an empty room in our house where, to my surprise, my father produced a bottle of Black Label Scotch whisky.

"How did you get whisky?" I asked with surprise.

"I have my contacts," my father said, using the same words that Jabar had used. "You have one glass to calm your nerve and a second to celebrate your wedding."

After that we went back to the square where my father directed me to sit in the prominent place chosen for the bridegroom. He went back to supervise the cooking and frequently came back to ask the guests if they needed anything. At 9 p.m., some teenagers came with *aftaba wa lagan* to pour water on the hands of each guest to wash them, and the *sofras* were laid. On top of these were placed a number of different foods, both meat and vegetables. My father had had three sheep slaughtered for the wedding and now the food was here in front of the guests, who were encouraged to eat beyond their limits. And they did. After the food, black and green tea arrived with sweets and then my favourite musician, Hamahang, started tuning his instruments and soon began to sing:

I am intoxicated with the beauty of your spring
Oh my beloved, where are you? Why are you running away?

Now it was time for calm and slow *ghazel* singing, not appropriate for dancing. Men listened quietly and nodded when a word from the mouth of the singer touched their heart. The celebrations continued but by 1 a.m. guests started leaving. Near 2 a.m., my father whispered in my ears to go to sleep because Jamila was waiting for me.

When I entered my bedroom, Jamila was sitting on the bed. I said salaam and sat next to her. She smiled and I smiled back, taking her right hand in both my hands, taking her *chador* from her face, looking at the beautiful henna designs on her hands. I brought her hands towards my nose and smelled the scent of henna, inhaling. And so began our married life.

Chapter 10

Studying at the Academy

The night before I went to Kabul I couldn't sleep because I had heard how tough the exam was. It had been difficult to get my mother to agree to me joining the army and now the fear of failing was preventing me from sleeping. In the morning, my mother made me an elaborate breakfast. Fortunately, my appetite was not affected by my tiredness and I ate as much as I could. Before leaving the house, my mother held a copy of the Quran over my head and asked me to step under it as I walked out of the house. Both my parents gave me a tight hug but I did not allow them to come with me to the bus stop. Four other boys from the surrounding villages were also going to Kabul and we were catching the bus together.

As I went into the exam room, I could feel the beating of my heart against my ribcage. I knew lack of sleep would affect my concentration. The room in the army academy building, which was more like a big hall, was bright because of the white paint and big windows. Rows of chairs with small desks attached to them were arranged in perfect lines and there were two corridors in the middle for exam invigilators and army officers, who were teaching at the academy, to walk and watch over the students: one group to make sure that no one cheated, the other consisting of teachers who were there to answer questions if someone did not understand the exam papers.

I was about forty-five minutes early and I took a seat. The room was cold, yet it was not a cold day. Thirty minutes before the exam, all the chairs were occupied. No one was going to arrive any later than that – we all had great respect for this exam. About fifteen minutes before the exam started, a professor explained the rules and told us that the questions were multiple choice. When I turned my paper over, my hand shook, but as I read the first question and circled the correct answer out of four and then the second and the third as well, I realised that I was well prepared for this exam.

To be eligible for the army exam, you had to have high marks in school, which I had. Because of that the exam was relatively easy for me. Sometimes I looked around to see what other participants did and noticed some pale faces, and people biting the end of their pens. I finished at least thirty minutes before the exam time was over and spent that time checking my answers once again. When I got out, Zaman, my school classmate who lived not far from my village, rushed towards me.

"Sons of bitches made the questions very hard," he said, looking at me to see what I was thinking.

"It wasn't bad," I said.

"Not bad? Those stupid questions about trigonometry."

"Well, the army uses trigonometry, as you know."

"What do I know about trigonometry? I thought the definition of a soldier was to take a gun and shoot with accuracy."

Zaman was in fact a good target shooter and we both practised target-shooting in Nijrab. But I hadn't realised that he believed all a soldier needed to know was how to use his gun.

Normally winters in Nijrab feel long because there is nothing to do in the village apart from waiting for the spring to come. But that winter was the longest, waiting for my exam results. We were told there would be an announcement on the radio after three months, but I wanted to know the result now and get it over with. What if I were the real fool, not understanding the questions, thinking they were easy? I heard an anecdote about an army general who was in a deep sleep when a soldier woke him up. The general opened his eyes in panic and asked the reason for such haste. The soldier said that the enemy was on the attack. The general replied, "I thought it was exam time." If I failed I would not be able to face my family or the villagers.

I told everyone I was going to be an army officer, not a doctor or an engineer. They would think I was an idiot. Too confident.

There was a man in our village who really liked me and stopped each time we met for a short chat. When I saw him on the path, he asked about my exam result and I asked why he was asking. Realising I was rude, I apologised. But my reaction was enough for the man to tell the other villagers that I had failed. Probably, he said it out of sympathy for me. When people showed sorrow for my failure, I told my father about it. He said, "Do you study for the people or for yourself?" After that I didn't pay attention and didn't even mention that the results had not been announced yet.

When Radio Afghanistan, the government radio station, announced that the results of the army academy exams were available on the notice boards of the academy, I could not sleep that night and I was the first passenger on the bus the following morning. Zaman did not have the same enthusiasm and came when the bus was half full. So did the other three guys. We all took a taxi together from the bus station in Kabul to the academy.

When I could not see my name on the list, I nearly collapsed.

"What is wrong?" Zaman said when he saw me squatting on the grass.

"My name is not on the list," I said.

"But that's not true, you're number forty-three."

"Please don't joke."

"Come and see it for yourself." He pulled me towards the notice board.

I had got the forty-third highest mark out of 5,000 students who had taken the exam. Only 550 places were available.

I immediately took a taxi to the bus station, catching a bus just minutes before its departure. When I got home and told my father, he invited many friends and villagers to celebrate. I don't know how he got his vodka or from where. He also invited the same man who had spread stories about my failure, not to embarrass him but to make sure he joined our happiness. After all, he was always kind to me.

On 19 March, I took a bus with my father to Kabul, initially to stay with one of our relatives, and then on 22 March I went to the army academy to register. My father knew about rules and the importance of being on time. The twenty-first of March is the Afghan new year's day, or *Nawrooz*. It might not have been possible to travel by bus on that day because people would be celebrating. The Taliban had banned *Nawrooz* celebrations, calling it un-Islamic. But as they'd disappeared, the people went wild, making up for lost time, celebrating, preparing days in advance.

The cancelation of *Nawrooz* by the Taliban had nothing to do with Islam. The Taliban were anti-happiness. They'd banned music, cinema and television, and in addition, parks were destroyed to be replaced by massive mosques. And yet half of Kabul was in ruins. They could have built their mosques in those places. They also converted cinemas to mosques.

Being away from family, friends and close relatives did not worry me and I was not bothered that I could not celebrate *Nawrooz* with them in Nijrab. In my heart there was another celebration, the celebration of following my father's footsteps to become an army officer. Would I be as good as him? Time would tell when I faced the bullet of the enemy.

My father was right. Some students missed the first day and our teachers were not happy about that. One of them said, "We teach you the art of defending your country. You cannot be late for one day while the enemy is approaching. Deal with the current situation as if you are at the front line."

From the first day we were told the rules. After morning prayer, which was before dawn, no one was allowed to sleep. The day then started with physical training. We jogged in two columns, carrying 10kg backpacks. We were divided into twenty groups and at the head of each group was an officer leading the march. Our officer, Commander Ashraf Khan from Badakhshan, was a tall Tajik with a bony face and a flat stomach. He was about 30 and, after a march of 5km, I did not see any sweat on his forehead. He was the fittest among all of us and that was because of jogging every morning. While I considered myself to be very fit, I had never run every morning in Nijrab. So learning from our leaders, my first goal was to run 5km with the others and not break a sweat. However, I noticed some boys could not continue no matter how hard Commander Ashraf Khan pushed them. Unfortunately, sixty-one students did not pass the physical test regardless of the result of their written test. One was a boy who was in fourteenth place. Despite that high mark, he had to go home.

After the morning physical training we all went for a shower. Sometimes, the shower was ice cold. That was for circulation and for enduring the cold. Then we had our breakfast, of which there was plenty, and it was very healthy too. Our government was feeding us well. At 8 a.m. sharp, and not even a second later, we all had to be present in our classes. For that reason we were there at least ten minutes early.

The teaching was strict and, exactly like a civilian university, we studied a range of subjects, such as maths, chemistry, physics, structure, and technical drawing for the first year. In the second year, students would be divided according to their plans to become doctors, lawyers or civil engineers.

Some students failed their exams and they were also sent home. At the end of three years, 471 students were left out of 550.

Lunch was at 1 p.m. sharp and lectures started again at 2 p.m. They continued until 5 p.m., when we had an hour's break before going to the canteen for dinner at 6 p.m. After dinner we had a choice of going for a walk or to our dormitories. Each dormitory housed ten soldiers in five bunkbeds. We were permitted to read, listen to music, or play cards or chess. My favourite game was chess but if I wanted to be by myself, I read a book. Listening to music was with headphones only. At 9 p.m. the lights went out and no one was allowed to use their mobile phones for any purpose. The room had to be completely silent because we needed our sleep.

Our day off started at 1 p.m. on Thursday, but before that lunch was served at noon. No one was allowed to leave the academy before lunch, and at 12:45 p.m., names were read out to make sure everyone was present. No one left before lunch anyway. One reason was the punishment. The other was the good food.

We had to be back before 5 p.m. on Friday. Anyone who came late or the following day would be punished by not being allowed to have a day off next week. So it was very rare that anyone did that. To make sure I had a good record, I never missed coming back before 5 p.m. on Fridays. My main motivation was that I loved army discipline, learning it from my father. He said, "The army makes you a man."

So when the officer shouted, "Amir, son of Masjidi," I shouted back, "Present." I then happily waited for my dinner at 6 p.m. I loved army food but to keep my mother happy, I told her I missed her chapati, which was true. The Kabuli naan was a poor replacement.

I thought we were the fittest people until I saw Captain William from the British Army. The reason I remember his name is because he made us write it many times and ensured he was referred to as Captain William, not captain or sir. He was masculine and slim. According to our culture if a man was not a bit fat, he was not healthy. But, by god, that man, at the age of 34, was the fittest among all of us. He said the reason was because even prior to joining the army, which made a soldier exercise every day, he went to the gym regularly, and when he joined the army, daily army training for him was a piece of cake. That is how I learned about this expression for the first time in my life, a piece of cake.

Every morning at exactly 6:30 a.m., twenty of us stood in front of him. Other groups had their own equivalent of Captain William. The morning exercises began after he first shouted good morning and we replied saying the same thing. We all learned how to say good morning in English. He was responsible for our physical training. When I told my father, he said, "In the history of our Afghan Army, we haven't had the kind of vigorous exercises you have and that means you are going to be more professional than I am. It is true because you are trained by the best army officers in the world, the British and the Americans." We had a list of exercises to follow:

1. Jumping jacks
2. Half-jumping jacks
3. Windmills
4. Two-count windmills
5. Trunk side stretch
6. Pull up series, consisting of close grip, wide grip, behind neck, regular grip
7. Push up series, consisting of dips, regular, triceps, wide grips, dive bomber
8. Variety of sit-ups, such as regular, cross arm, half-sit-ups, cruncher sit-ups, automatic sit-ups
9. Flutter kicks
10. Lizard stretch
11. Neck rotation while lying on the stomach, with head up, both clockwise and anticlockwise
12. Neck left
13. Different types of squatting
14. Charlie Chaplins (he had to explain that this exercise was named after a great movie star, who often stood on his toes and then shifted his legs to be supported by his soles)

While many of us could not keep up with Captain William, he was doing all the exercises in front of us on a platform so we could see him. But he always gave us breaks between sets and made sure we all drank water. If someone could not keep up, he would shout, "Drink water, soldier. Then do your exercise."

Once a month we had a special operation very similar to what was happening in the field facing the enemy, something like target-shooting or bringing a make believe injured soldier to safety. These operations happened during the day time and on that day we did not study. However, to test our endurance, and to learn how to cope with mental fatigue, we took part in night operations too.

One Wednesday, Commander Hanif, my favourite officer, summoned all the soldiers together and read out the names of

100 students. He told the remaining students to go back to their classes. My name was on that list of 100 students.

"Listen up," he shouted. "You have been chosen for a special operation which starts at 7 p.m. when it is dark. You will all bring a 10kg-pack of different things, such as your tent, tinned food, water bottles and whatever you think you will need when you are trying to find your way back to this base. You will be organised into groups of twenty students and you will be dropped by armoured vehicles within a 30km-radius. There will be no tarmac road but terrain hard enough for the armoured vehicles to travel on. Please put your names on your mobile phones and put them in this bag – they will only be returned to you when you reach this base. That way, no one will be able to use their mobile phones to help them find their way.

"Of course you will all be searched before your departure in case some of you have two mobile phones. We will also check that you are not carrying less than 10kg on your back. Please do not cheat because this exercise is to prepare you for real conditions, which will be much more difficult physically and mentally because you will be in real danger, facing an enemy who might find you before you get to safety. You are expected to return to your base by 1 a.m. If you do not reach here by that time, it is better not to, because those who come back to the comfort of their beds will be marked down. So I advise you to camp. I also advise you to keep a diary and let us know how you operate during this time. Remember, no matter how hard you think it is, the real operation in the field will be much tougher. Those who make it before 1 a.m. will have a high score according to their time and that score will go towards the mark that will mean they can proceed to the next year. I wish you all good luck."

That evening we had our dinner at 5 p.m. and by 6 p.m., we were all sitting in armoured vehicles. One hundred students were going to be dispatched to different parts of the countryside, 30km away from our base. Our two vehicles dropped us in the foothills in complete darkness at about 7:30 p.m. Our company of twenty students started moving, but I suggested that we must have one leader and one assistant leader and only these two could decide in which direction we would go or what we would do. Because of my suggestion, the company agreed that I would be the leader and I was allowed to choose my deputy. I chose Najaf, who was a Hazara, because those people were famous for strength and endurance.

Before our group moved again I suggested we go in one direction to reach a tarmac road, where we would hopefully see a sign that would show us the way back to Kabul. I also told them to watch out for any lights because that would be a sign there was a house. My group voted that we go right. The reason I asked my group members to vote was because I did not want to take the blame if we ended up going the wrong way.

No one complained about the speed at which we were walking as we were all fit following our army exercises every morning. The half-moon gave us enough light to see our steps. After an hour, we reached a stream.

"We walk downstream," I shouted.

"Why?" Najaf asked.

"Because there is a good chance that along the stream we'll encounter a village or reach a tarmac road."

They all agreed and continued walking downstream. In my heart I was praying that none of my group members fell and got injured because carrying an injured man with us would slow us down. And yet I urged them to walk faster, which increased the chance of falling. I was at the front and Najaf at the back. I had the task of pulling and Najaf was responsible for pushing. But for now there was no need for this because we had not walked for long.

Stars were bright and the cool breeze on a hot August night was welcoming. We were all quiet as if we were hiding from the enemy. But this part of Afghanistan was safe. The quietness was part of our training. The only sounds were the stream and the cicadas. The terrain was rough, not like the countryside of Nijrab, with no vegetation and no sign of life. At that moment I thought of the nights in Nijrab when I walked on the path alongside green fields, listening to the hissing sound of the night and the sound of the river nearby. In August, the crops in the cornfields were more than a metre high, mulberries hung in trees, walnuts were big, hanging in their green shells and, of course, there was the scent of the oleaster tree, which my mother warned me was dangerous because poisonous snakes had nests under them. Apparently, they also liked the heavenly scent. But here it seemed like a different planet. My country had a diverse climate and landscape:

Amidst rolling fields of emerald green,
where nature's beauty reigns,
unseen beauty of Nijrab stretched, tranquil and wide,
where time moved slow and peace resided.
Whispering winds through ancient trees,
a symphony of birds, melodies to please.
Golden sunsets, painting skies aglow,
in rural realms, where dreams can grow.
Rural mud built houses, with gardens fair,
wild flowers dancing in the summer air.
Babbling brooks and meadows wide.
The scent of earth after gentle rain,
a simpler life, free from city's strain,
in rural beauty, a world apart,
a sanctuary for a weary heart.

We were stationed in Kabul, which was hot in the summer. But if we went to Paghman Valley, just forty-five minutes by car from our base, we could see mountaintops still covered with white snow, even in August. The rivers were freezing cold, because their sources were melted ice and snow. When it snowed in Kabul in the winter, only a two-hour drive away, you would reach Jalalabad, where you would be greeted with tropical weather. Tall cypress trees lined the tarmac road, huge palm and *neem* trees in the garden, monkeys jumping from one branch to another. And we had our deserts, the biggest one Helmand

Desert. Helmand was still the power house of the Taliban and from time to time they appeared on the streets, causing skirmishes. But they were not strong enough to be a threat to the government. They were in the mountains and the deserts and, at that moment, when I walked in a safe place with my nineteen comrades, I thought of what would happen if I was alone in that desert or on that mountain, surrounded by the Taliban, trying to find my way to safety. Being in the army was not like the hide and seek I played with my friends in the cornfields, shooting each other with wooden sticks, pretending to be injured and then, as if nothing was happening, getting up and shooting the enemy. Even here, on this mission, what would happen if I got it wrong and this stream ended up nowhere? My comrades would blame me for a bad decision and getting them low marks. But in the fighting field, I knew one wrong decision would end up in lost lives. My father had told me many stories about his right and wrong judgements in the army and how he learned from them, so for me this exercise was as my officers had designed it: an experience to learn from and become a good soldier.

We were delighted to reach a dark tarmac road on which cars occasionally passed. Some of the students suggested we stop one of the cars and ask for directions, but I did not agree. I thought it was cheating and also feared that our officers might have planted a spy in our group. Anyway, for me, scoring high or low was not important anymore. We had things to learn from this exercise.

By the time we reached the road we had been in the open for one and a half hours. I gathered my group together. "We have a choice – we can go right or left. The chances are we will reach a signpost either way directing us to Kabul."

"But what happens if the signpost appears after twenty kilometres?"

"In that case we camp until daylight. We have been very lucky to discover this tarmac road and you know real fighting conditions are not like this."

"You already sound like an army officer, Amir," one of them joked, and they all laughed.

“I am afraid from now on we will need to jog. Please don’t lose hope, we will still have a chance to reach our base before one.”

As luck had it, after about thirty minutes we reached a crossroads and on it the direction for Kabul was given. We were 20km away. Of course, once we reached the outskirts of Kabul, we still had to proceed to our base. But that was not a problem. Once we neared Kabul, we knew how to find our base. I consulted Najaf and asked him about the strength of our group. There was one student who, due to illness, had not slept well and had difficulty following with the rest. Immediately, without losing time, I ordered that his backpack should be emptied and distributed among the others. Fortunately, they all agreed and there were two very strong students who took more weight than the others.

“Listen up, now we have a good chance to reach our base before the deadline. But we must speed up. Hamid is ill and needs help, one of you must look after him.”

“Hamid is my friend, Amir. I’ll help and, if need be, I’ll carry him,” said Munir, another strong student from the Hazara region of Afghanistan. These Hazaras could carry loads up to their own weight for a long distance. Fearing that we would fail to reach Kabul in time and that we would get low marks, the students put all their energy into running. I told them that from time to time we would have a three-minute break for water and a rest. As for myself, I was in perfect shape and loved the challenge. In the past I had also carried big sacks of flour from the flour mill, sometimes up to 40kg.

We reached Kabul just an hour before time and from there to our base was a smooth ride. Just eleven minutes before 1 a.m. we reached our base and each one of us went directly to their beds, collapsing. We were allowed to sleep until nine in the morning. That night I slept as if the world did not exist. I was exhausted and I was sure my team had the same feeling. After taking a cold shower to wake me up, I went to have breakfast, which I thought for the first time was not enough. During our breakfast, we found out that our group was the fourth fastest. After us, another group entered the base just six minutes before time. Five groups had to spend the night outside the base.

After breakfast, I went with my team to an empty classroom where two officers, Kamal Khan and Mohsen Khan, were waiting for us.

"We would like to know how you managed to get back to this base and, beside that, your strategy."

I got up and started explaining.

"Sir, immediately after we were dropped off by the vehicles, we decided to select a leader and a deputy."

"Who suggested this?" Kamal Khan asked.

"We all did," I said, knowing it was a positive act. I wanted all my team to get a credit for it.

"Normally one guy suggests that but I accept your explanation," Mohsen Khan said.

"And who was the leader," Kamal Khan asked.

"They voted I should be the leader and I chose a deputy."

"On what basis did you choose your deputy and who was he?" Kamal Khan asked.

"I chose Najaf because I have been watching how effortlessly he completed the morning exercises." I looked at Najaf and saw him smiling at me.

"That is a good point, soldier, to observe each other." Kamal Khan started writing in his notebook.

"Najaf stand up!" Mohsen Kahn shouted. Najaf stood.

"Were you happy with your leader, Najaf?" Mohsen Khan asked.

"One hundred per cent, sir."

"But why? You are the strongest man in the group. You should have been the leader."

"I was given a task at that moment and the issue of leadership was not important. The most important issue for us was to come back safely." Kamal Khan's head went down and his pen moved over the notebook.

"And what was your contribution?"

"I was at the rear of the line urging my men to go fast and sometimes I even pushed them forward."

"Okay, sit down, Najaf. So how did you begin, Amir?"

I told them the whole story of finding the stream and after that the tarmac road and so on.

"I am sure on that tarmac road you encountered pedestrians and vehicles and you could have asked for directions." Mohsen looked into my eyes, deadly serious.

"Indeed we encountered vehicles, but we wanted to make the experience like a real task, something we might encounter in the battlefield." Again I noticed Kamal Khan writing.

"One last question." Mohsen Khan raised his voice. "Did you encounter any problems?"

"Hamid was ill and we decided to carry his load."

"Excellent, soldier." Mohsen clapped. "It is very important for a soldier to feel he is not only responsible for his own life but for the lives of his comrades too. One day you might have to carry an injured soldier in the battlefield. Good work and you are dismissed."

I noticed Kamal Khan's pen speeding over the paper again. At that moment I did not know that one day I would have to carry an injured comrade while his blood soaked the back of my shirt.

Chapter 11

After the Academy, March 2014

The Afghan Army was approximately divided in the following manner:

1. Qol-e Urdu, consisting of 20,000 to 30,000 soldiers
2. Lowa, consisting of 3,500 to 5,000 soldiers
3. Kandak, consisting of 400 to 800 soldiers
4. Tolai, consisting of 60 to 100 soldiers
5. Blook, consisting of 35 to 50 soldiers
6. Delgai, consisting of 10 to 15 soldiers

The smallest division was Kandak, which consisted of between 500 to 1,200 soldiers and officers. Afghanistan had nine Qol-e Urdu and the army was based in four zones: Northern, Southern, Eastern and Western zone. All of these Qol-e Urdus and zones were situated outside the cities and because of their size each Qol-e Urdu resembled a big town.

After studying for three years, I became a junior officer but before I was dispatched to a Qol-e Urdu, I was sent to Darulaman base in Kabul for a further six months to learn how to use different weapons designed for the infantry – following in my father's footstep. The weapons I learned to use included:

1. M2.50 Calibre Machine-gun
2. M142 High Mobility Artillery Rocket System (HIMARS)
3. MK19 Grenade Machine-gun
4. M16A2 5.56 Rifle
5. M4 Carbine

6. Beretta M9 Pistol
7. M224 60mm Mortar
8. FGM-148 Javelin
9. XM25 Counter Defilade Target Engagement System
10. M252 Mortar
11. MK16 SCAR
12. M72 Light Anti-Armour Weapon (LAW)
13. M107 50 Calibre Long-Range Sniper Rifle (LRSR)
14. M240B
15. M249 Squad Automatic
16. XM2010 Enhanced Sniper Weapon

My officers noticed I had a talent for being a sniper and for that reason I was given an enhanced sniper rifle. I was very pleased and proud to carry this weapon on my shoulder.

My father was not pleased when he learned that I was posted in Urozgan, one of the least secure places in Afghanistan, but none of us could do anything about it. The dispatch of fresh army graduates was based on a lottery. An army officer picked out the names from a bowl.

Even before the wars, and at the time that the country enjoyed peace under the rule of King Mohammad Zahir Shah, people said, "If you want to die, go to Urozgan." Because of its harsh climate, unsuitable for living, it was the least developed of all provinces and populated by the least educated people, who lived in absolute poverty. Only some districts had a small patch of greenery, the rest were all barren and it seemed that nothing could grow there. We have provinces like Kapisa, Parwan and Badakhshan where everywhere is green and covered in vegetation, and then there are provinces like Helmand and Urozgan that are almost barren. The harsh landscape and climate affected the people, and they too were harsh, ready to kill or be killed, with very little value for life. When you have no life, you might as well be dead. That was why these provinces were the stronghold of the Taliban. If you die, you don't lose anything. This kind of a person can be very dangerous to encounter in the battlefield.

For the first time in its history, Afghanistan had a professional army. Our soldiers were not conscripts who had not even seen a gun in their lives. Now we received training from the best armies in the world, the Americans and the British. I graduated with a recommendation from the army academy and when I went home to tell my father, he went to the market the following day and bought a lamb for slaughtering, inviting friends and villagers to celebrate.

Urozgan is very close to Helmand and Qandahar, the two hot spots of the Taliban. I thought that if I wanted to become a proper soldier, Urozgan was the right place because life was threatened by both the harsh environment and the cruel enemy.

All together there were 4,300 soldiers and army officers. There were six Kandaks or battalions, each consisting of up to 800 soldiers. Two of our Kandaks, Kandak 4 and 5, were based in our compound and I belonged to Kandak 5. My responsibility was guarding our compound and securing our area. Our other three battalions were based in the troubled districts of Urozgan province.

While the Taliban did not have the strength to attack us face to face, they used long-range weapons, firing rockets from a distance. Our supplies for food came directly from Kabul by plane, but when planes failed to arrive soldiers had to go to Qandahar in a convoy of armoured vehicles. This was the most dangerous task, because along the road the Taliban had placed mines and ambushed us. Basically, they attacked, destroying armoured vehicles, hoping to kill some of us and then disappear. However, later on when the Taliban became stronger, such attacks were regarded as skirmishes, just to scare soldiers.

The difficulty with retaliating was that the Taliban launched rockets from one place but as soon as we located the place where the rocket had come from, they moved. Or they fired from civilian houses knowing if we returned fire we would risk killing innocent people. Our enemy was a coward and used innocent people as a shield.

Two days before our food supplies ran out, the commander of my Kandak summoned me.

"Amir! The plane bringing our food supplies has not come this week. This time you will be the commander of ten armoured vehicles. Select your soldiers to go to Qandahar with you, in total forty of them. This mission will give you good experience out of this compound."

"I will do it, sir."

"I am glad, but ask other officers who have carried out this mission before about the journey. Make yourself familiar."

I asked officers who'd taken this journey before and they told me that it was like a lottery. Sometimes the enemy was there and sometimes not, because they didn't know exactly when we ran out of food and needed to travel to Qandahar. For them it was also logistically difficult to stay in one place without being certain. Beside choosing nine armoured vehicles, I also chose one army tank. Officers thought I was panicking too much and that was not necessary because the tank moved slowly and that would have an impact on the length of journey. But I told them since it was my mission and I was the commander, I would do whatever I thought was necessary to make sure my soldiers travelled safely. I also asked for at least one radio to be provided for each vehicle in case we were attacked so that we could communicate with each other.

With my favourite sniper weapon M24 in hand, wearing my best helmet, I stood at the commander hatch of the tank, choosing to be in the first vehicle. The other nine vehicles, at a distance of 5m between them, followed me. For about an hour nothing happened. A few cars came from the opposite direction or overtook us. The only noise on the tarmac was the noise of our tyres and the screeching of the army tank on the road. But I was watching the whole 180 degrees around us. In the past our convoy had consisted of fast armoured vehicles speeding up to reach their destination and when they were attacked they did not respond but just noted the location of the attack and reported it to the base.

My head was boiling because of the heat of the hot sun making the helmet hot. Sweat streamed down the back of my neck, all the way to waist of my trousers. *Bang!* A bullet missed my helmet but hit the commander's hatch. I went down, radioed the others and ordered them to shoot in the direction the bullets were coming from, which was a ruined building. The Taliban were behind the half-destroyed mud walls. We could not see their faces but could see the barrels of their guns. Our armoured vehicles had windows from which my soldiers could shoot. They were shooting non-stop, but no vehicle moved forward, which was in contrast to the past. I ordered the man in charge of the tank gun to turn the head of the gun towards the ruined building and shoot, a risk I was prepared to take even though there could have been innocent civilians in the ruins. Because of the war and extreme poverty, ordinary people lived in ruins and I was praying in my heart that this was not the case there. The tank fired four times and then I told the man responsible to stop because half of the ruins had gone. For a long time the enemy responded, hitting the metal of our vehicles. But immediately after they stopped firing at us, I ordered the drivers of our vehicles to approach the ruin. When we got there, we saw the bodies of the dead Taliban fighters. There must have been more of them but the rest had escaped.

We reached Qandahar without further incident. Qandahar was the capital during the reign of Emperor Ahmad Shah Durani, who ruled over the whole of today's Afghanistan as well as half of Iran and India. But as is the nature of the Afghans, after his early death at the age of 50, his grandsons started fighting each other for the throne and that gave an opportunity for the British and the Sikhs to take land from Afghanistan in India. The Iranians also managed to get their land back. The British not only took India from Afghanistan but Afghanistan came under British rule. However, once the capital of the great emperor, Qandahar was still the second largest after Kabul, with well-planned residential areas, tarmac roads, an international airport, cafés and restaurants. I ordered my men to pack as much food as possible in our ten army vehicles, making sure to have enough food if the plane delivering food from Kabul to Urozgan did not return. Then I let my soldiers loose to enjoy being in Qandahar for a day, knowing that during the war soldiers needed entertainment. I'd read how the British and Americans brought singers and entertainers to army camps during the Second World War, not far from the front lines.

A famous Pashto singer, Alam Gul, was giving a concert in Qandahar football stadium and my soldiers decided to go there. They also insisted that I accompany them. I'd never been to any concert of a Pashto singer, but to show my soldiers that I shared happiness with them, I went. Fortunately, the security was well organised, making sure there was no one from the Taliban blowing himself up, killing innocent people while the concert was taking place. The stadium was packed and Alam Gul appeared on stage with his five band members about thirty minutes late. The band consisted of keyboard, *tabla*, *dhul*, harmonium and flute players. Alam Gul started singing happy songs and soon the audience were on their feet, dancing. My soldiers also joined in, dancing *atan*, the nation's popular dance, and they pulled me up to join them. We danced until we were exhausted and although I could not understand what Alam Gul was singing because I do not speak Pashto, I thoroughly enjoyed the concert.

Fortunately, on the way back we did not encounter the enemy. After two hours we reached the base, and the commander of our Lowa summoned me.

"How was your trip?" Major General Azim Khan asked.

"It was good, sir."

"Any trouble?"

"Just a little."

"It wasn't just a little, lieutenant, I know the whole story. A commander of Lowa must know about every mission big and small."

"Well, sir, when we were travelling, after an hour into our journey we were ambushed and we responded."

"Normally when the enemy fires on a logistic convoy, the convoy speeds up to get out of trouble."

"Sir! The enemy was hiding behind the walls of a ruined building and they were shooting at us. I knew this had happened in the past when I asked other officers about the journey. In the past our convoys did not have a tank with them. This time, with the help of the tank, we hit back and destroyed those walls. We also killed six Taliban."

"You could have easily killed twenty civilians with your actions."

"This ruined building was far away from any village. The reason the Taliban hid behind the walls and shot at us in the past was because the mud walls were strong and when my colleagues in the past responded with machine-gunfire, it was not effective. So I used the tank and destroyed the walls. In the future the enemy will not have those walls to hide behind and attack us. That is why on the way back we had no trouble."

"But you even followed the enemy."

"Not really. We just went up to the ruin to check no one from the enemy side was left."

"Officer, I admire your courage but taking risks must be well calculated. We are always criticised by ordinary people for taking risks that end in losing civilian lives. Our enemy hides behind civilians. Taking the risk to attack the enemy from a distance was fine because the place was not near a village. But to go to the ruin was too risky. You know that sometimes the enemy sends small numbers of fighters to draw us into combat, and then from nowhere a bigger number appears with anti-tank and anti-armour vehicles. Once again I admire your courage, but you may not take as much risk in the future."

"Yes, sir."

"Since you did well, you will be the leader of such missions in the future."

I was happy with the result of our mission and the assessment received. For some months, the route from Urozgan to Qandahar was safe.

Right: We needed good protection against a mad enemy who did not value even his own life.

Below: Lining up with new graduates at the academy where I studied to become a commando.

Above left: Constantly watching for an enemy who would often appear from nowhere.

Above right: Addressing new graduates.

Above: With Commander Basir Andarabi after a bloody battle. Our ambulance was destroyed by a road bomb.

Below left: Head of battalion awarding Commander Basir Andarabi the medal of honour for his bravery.

Above: Commander Basir Andarabi gives instruction. He was well respected.

Below: Basir Andarabi in civilian life.

Commando Especial Force ready for combat.

Above left: Commander Basir Andarabi.

Above middle: Zabihullah Kohsar, commander of local forces in Nijrab, who fought the Taliban after the fall of the Afghan Government. He was later killed in battle by the Taliban.

Above right: Assadullah Shamal, brother of Zabihullah Kohsar, who was commander of the local police. Like his brother he continued fighting the Taliban after the fall of the Afghan Government and was later killed by the Taliban.

Above: General Akmal Amir.

Left: We held our positions, sometimes without food or water.

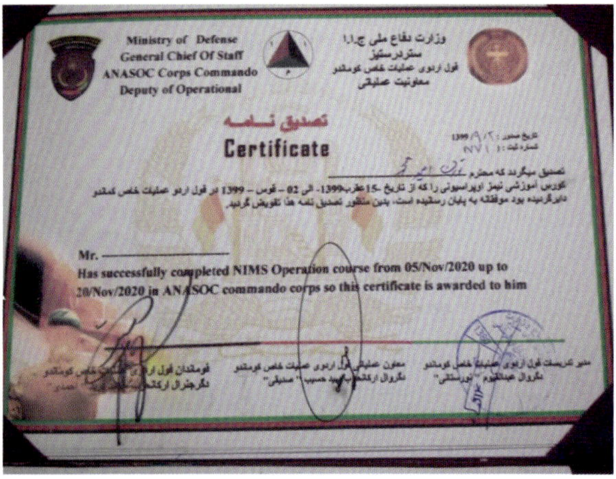

Above: After capturing the Taliban base we captured their flag, but as a verse from the Quran is on it, we could not drop it on the floor.

Left: A certification of appreciation for my effort fighting the Taliban, given to me by the leader of our battalion, General Ahmadzai, in Helmand.

After defeating the Taliban, we discovered a room in which they had been making bombs.

While the Taliban either killed or tortured those they captured, we treated them with humanity.

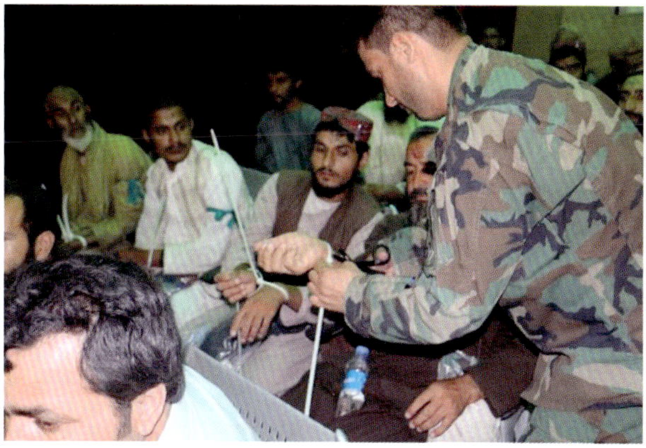

We gave the Taliban food and showed them respect.

Mullah Wakil, a captured Taliban commander.

Above left: Commander Khalid Nijrabi, later killed in action by the Taliban.

Above right: The Taliban hid in civilian houses from where they attacked us, knowing we could not respond because we did not want innocent people to lose their lives. They also wore women's clothes when they entered our compounds with bombs and other weapons.

Above left: Taliban at night.

Above right: Captured Taliban dressed in women's clothes, with 'her' gun.

With our American friends among the villagers.

Right: An American soldier who learned our language is reading for the children.

Below left: We joked and laughed with American officers when we relaxed.

Below right: Afghan ladies buying fabric.

Listening to our leaders with the locals.

Our officers lost their legs due to an anti-personnel mine.

Ready to take on the enemy.

Village children loved talking with American soldiers.

Chapter 12

Helmand

Whenever I saw the US Marines in our compound in Urozgan, I noticed they were a different breed. The way they walked and talked, and the way they carried their guns. It was all different. None of them were fat and they all had cheekbones. I loved their sunglasses and I imagined that they could see through those glasses much more than we could see with our naked eyes, imagining that those sunglasses told them who was friend and who was foe. Their uniform was also different from the rest. Trying to look like them, I also bought expensive sunglasses and guarded them with my life, fearing that someone might steal them from me. But just pretending to be a marine was not enough. So I told my father about my desire to become a commando, a member of the Afghan special forces. My father said it was a good idea but the exam was very difficult.

Once my father gave me permission to become a commando, I made enquiries. Fortunately one distant relative was already a commando and I decided to meet him when my leave came around because he was in Mazar-e Sharif, north of Afghanistan, about six hours drive. Halim, a man three years older than me, was already known to us in Nijrab for his strength, politeness and also his educational achievements. He was a down-to-earth person and when I met him in Mazar-e Sharif, he showed incredible kindness and generosity, encouraging me to take the exam. He described and explained the physical test and gave me as much information as he could regarding the written test. He said the test focused on maths, physics and geography, and there were some questions related to battle issues. In his test he was asked how he would continue resisting the enemy while his compound was surrounded and there was a shortage of food. Reinforcements were at least four days away and the enemy knew that if the reinforcements came the battle would be lost, so they continued intensifying the fight. He said to answer such a question I must use my imagination because there was no fixed answer for it. I did not ask what his answer was but the question made me think for some days. How could you survive in those circumstances? One thing I was sure about was not to panic, because when a soldier panics, the battle is lost.

Beside daily exercises I did further training to increase my fitness, and the only time available to do that was between Thursday and Friday when we had a break or in the evening after dinner. Just an hour after dinner I started my own exercises as if I were a boxing champion getting ready for a big fight. When I went home on Thursdays, once again I followed my strict regime of exercising, which upset my mother. She told me I had no time to be with her but my father was encouraging me to do even more, knowing my dream. Finally I managed to sit the exam and I passed both the written and physical tests. I was posted to Helmand.

My father had once told me about the paradise called Helmand and had shown me photos of miles and miles of green fields, the bread basket of Afghanistan. In the 1960s, our king, Mohammad Zahir Shah, convinced the US government to build a huge dam on the Helmand River called Kajaki. The purpose was to convert a massive part of the Helmand desert into farmland. The project took more than ten years. During this time, American engineers settled in Helmand with their wives and children. Their settlement was designed exactly like a settlement in Texas, with gardens boasting lawns, flowers and palm trees. Now that water was available, they also built a good-sized swimming pool. Their wives and children used the pool when the men went to work on the Helmand project. They had their own church and school. Afghan engineers who studied in the US lived with their families in the same place. Their children went to the same American school, and were educated in the English language. These children one day would become bilingual engineers and doctors. Some would go to the US after winning scholarships. There were mixed marriages too, just like in the novel written by James Mitchener, *The Caravan*, in which an Afghan engineer falls in love with an American woman who has come to Afghanistan. In that novel, Helmand is a very scary place where caravans get lost and people die. The novel describes the Afghanistan of a century ago when there were no roads and caravans were used for commerce and travelling. My father had read that novel in translation and told me about it. But the Americans changed that harsh land into a paradise, only to become a land of poison during the reins of the Mujahideen and the Taliban.

When no country apart from Pakistan recognised the Taliban regime after the Mujahideen were defeated, the Taliban, not receiving any financial support and with no trade with the outside world, actively encouraged farmers in Helmand to grow poppies, and opium became the main export to Pakistan, ignored by the corrupt government there. The Pakistan government even made money out of it. I wanted to work with the US soldiers to change that land of poison back to paradise.

Helmand base, built around an airport, was a town in itself, with a circumference that would take a car travelling at 40 miles per hour an hour and a half to complete. Its outside wall was built of strong concrete. It was about 3m high and had 6m-high watchtowers at a distance of 100m. Two hundred metres inside that first wall was another wall, designed so that if the enemy passed the first wall, they would be caught at the second.

The gates were manned by plenty of armed men and there were two long-range M249 machine-guns on both sides. Inside, the buildings were made of connected containers similar to mobile homes. Around these buildings, some as long as 100m, once again were watchtowers, making sure those who worked or slept in the barracks were safe. We had a cinema, canteens for food and drink and a well-equipped hospital with doctors and nurses. We were in the Shuraba district, which means 'salty water' district. Perhaps in the past it had salty water but now, apart from our base located in a desert, the rest of the district was all green.

To entertain the army, famous artists were sometimes invited. I saw the concert of a famous singer, Popal. The Taliban had banned music when they ruled the country but now Afghanistan had many television channels. One had a popular show called *Afghan Star*. Popal was the finalist and was loved by both young women and men. Half of his popularity was due to his long hair and good looks.

After six months training in a commando camp, learning techniques from US and Royal Commando Marines, I became deputy to the commander of our Tolai, leading a unit of 120 trained soldiers. After several days I was given an assignment with Commander Basir Andarabi, who was the commander of the Tolai. In a short period, Commander Basir and I became very close friends and since Nijrab and Andarab had the same climate, nature and were both mainly occupied by Tajik people, we had many common things to talk about, such as agriculture, the way of life, and in addition to that we were both married and deeply in love with our wives. Commander Basir Andarabi had three children. Each time he went to Andarab he brought mulberries and walnuts back for me and when I went to Nijrab I brought pine nuts. What I loved the most I wanted to share with my good friend. Basir had already been on many missions and he told me how to fight and protect myself. But before getting out of the compound, our battle had to be well-planned, and that was with the assistance of the US and UK Marines.

For days we practised fighting in our compound where a huge ruin was built for us, similar to what we would encounter on the battlefield. Pointing a gun with one hand and holding a radio in the other, we turned and twisted, jumped over the walls, hiding, shooting. And we were made fully aware that the enemy had received good training from Arab terrorists based in Pakistan. They were born with weapons, an extra effort for their mothers to push them out, so they were soldiers from the time they opened their eyes to the world. They also knew the geography of the place because they lived there and could easily hide among the civilians, carrying spades or other farming tools pretending they were farmers. There was a fear deep within me too, but mine was different. Although Commander Andarabi had become my good friend, I was going on a mission with an experienced commander who had been hardened by commanding so many battles. My fear was related to my failure. This was another test. Obviously, if I failed I would be kept in the same position. But I wanted to go further, becoming commander of a Kandak in charge of 600–1,200 soldiers, meeting even more challenging tasks.

From Shurabak to our Lowa in Sangin, we had to go by Chinook helicopter because it was a long way. Once we landed at Lowa, we had to walk for about three hours to where the Kandak under attack was located in Sangin district. Sangin was one of the largest districts in our country. For the first time I was sat inside a giant Chinook. The inside was big enough to carry army tanks and other armoured vehicles. I observed our soldiers, some of them smiling nervously. Like me it was their first flight. As the helicopter took off I could clearly see the fear of flying on some of their faces. To make their fear disappear, I got up, started dancing, and pulled the hand of a soldier to join me. Some others joined and we danced and laughed to get the fear of flight and our dreadful coming combat out of our minds. Commander Basir laughed and told me it was a perfect way to relax our soldiers.

A marine had been watching me from the cockpit and kept smiling at my initiative of dancing to make the soldiers calm. He nodded and I realised that he was inviting me to come to the cockpit. I could not speak a word of English but there at the cockpit he pointed to the land below, a magnificent green paradise, in contrast to our base located in a desert. Was he telling me that it was the American engineers who converted that desert to a paradise? I am sure he was aware of that. I was embarrassed. People from his country came to change a desert where caravans disappeared into a farming land, and now snakes from my own country lived in it, cultivating the poison of opium. In my mind there were poisonous snakes hidden under the trees and bushes and I had the task of saving this land to make it safe for our boys and girls to go to school. One day they'd become engineers and build more dams and canals. We had many rivers that ended in deserts, one near Nijrab. President Daud Khan had a plan to build a big dam for agriculture and electricity in Nijrab, but then the civil war started and such projects were stopped. I wanted to know why people did not want to send their children to school but wished to change the farming land back to a desert. Were they happy to live in hunger and poverty? If yes, what was the reason for it?

After landing at the compound of our Lowa, we met General Latif, a well-qualified army officer who had spent two years in Sangin. He not only knew the geography of the area but also had a significant knowledge of the people and their customs. We were among the warrior race who, since their history began and since childhood, carried weapons. For them to be killed was more honourable than dying in their beds. Dying in bed was for women. When they did not have a common enemy, they were the enemies of their cousins and even brothers. There was always some kind of dispute to kill someone or to be killed. They did not solve their disputes through government law but through the elders of their villages. Animosity was carried for years between families and if a person was killed by member of a different family, one person from that family must be killed and then retaliation continued and killings made the ground red.

Three days before our departure, drones traversed Sangin district in order for us to learn the geography. While a drone was flying from one corner of Sangin district to another, we were in a big room with the US Marines, watching the area on a television screen. We could see the movement of the Taliban from one house to another. They had taken these houses from the villagers, pretending to be ordinary farmers, and we had the task of identifying which house belonged to a genuine farmer and which one to a Taliban fighter. There was no room for mistakes. If we got it wrong, we would be responsible for the death of innocent people who wanted to be protected. As a result, the Taliban would use our mistake, telling the locals that we were their enemy. We knew that no battle could be won without the support of the local people. For that reason we identified each house and numbered them on paper. Printouts were made available for both Basir and myself. The plan was that we would reach Sangin with forty-eight soldiers. To make sure that no one from our soldiers was a Taliban informer, we kept our plans secret. We were aware that Taliban were trying to infiltrate the army by bribing soldiers and even officers. One brigade commander would have been recruited by the Taliban if he'd accepted a bribe of $100,000, which is a huge amount of money. But the commander, who was an honest man, refused and informed the government about the use of such techniques. In that room, only Basir and I from the Afghan side were present. The rest were American advisers who talked to us through a translator.

We had informed our soldiers that we were going to a different district because they could inform the Taliban with their mobile phones the moment we left our Lowa's compound. At 2 a.m., when it was raining heavily, we started moving and our plan could not be changed. In fact the rain might have been an asset, keeping the Taliban away. As the Taliban had mined the road, we walked in the desert.

The main objective of the mission was to open the Taliban blockade, making sure our Kandak, consisting of 700 soldiers and officers, were able to receive food and arms, and also to bring the bodies of soldiers killed by the Taliban to our Lowa.

Under the darkness, and when the rain was still heavy, we started our journey. Fortunately, the desert is made of a combination of sand and soil, hard enough to walk on. We instructed our soldiers not to use army torches because the enemy could see us, and also told them they could not talk. We had to walk in the dark and in silence. In orderly single-file, I was at the rear of the line while Commander Basir walked at the front. We had also informed our base in Sangin in advance so that they would know we were coming, to make sure there was no friendly fire. With our backpacks and our M4s on our shoulders, we carried loads of about 15kg each. But we'd had enough training to carry such a load for a three-hour walk without any trouble.

It was a dark, quiet night without a single star in the sky, but we could still see our way parallel to the main road at the distance of half a kilometre to make sure that car drivers would not spot us. Fortunately, at that time of the night, no car was on the road and since the area was not safe because of the presence of the Taliban, not many cars dared to travel even during the day. The rain did not affect us because our clothes were waterproof and we wore hard helmets. In fact, it was more pleasant than a sunny day when the sun was hot and walking under it more difficult.

Without incident we reached Sangin Kandak at 5 a.m. We radioed our army unit, who opened the gate for us, all in a very quiet manner because we knew that the Taliban were nearby. In no time, the commander of the Kandak, a young man about my age called Esmat Khan, came to us and hugged both Commander Andarabi and me. From his welcome, I guessed how desperate he was and how pleased he was to see us.

He told us that the night was a good choice to walk because the Taliban blockade would not spot us. But if we came with army vehicles, they would have realised who we were and opened fire. They also shot helicopters down, so for us to come by helicopter was not possible either. Not only were our soldiers suffering from hunger because helicopters could not bring food, but their compound was flooded because the Taliban had diverted a stream into the compound.

Commander Nasim, the head of Sangin Kandak, welcomed us. From first sight I noticed that, despite constant attack by the Taliban, his morale was high. A leader must have high spirits to make sure his soldiers do not panic. He informed us that three of his soldiers had been killed and they needed to be taken to our Lowa, but before that he suggested we rest and eat breakfast, which we welcomed. We wanted our soldiers to be fresh before facing the Taliban that day.

By the time we left Sangin Kandak's base, the day was warm but not hot. We were provided with army Jeeps, but not armoured vehicles that would make us vulnerable to Taliban snipers, the best in the world. But we had no choice. We'd brought a team of mine-clearing personnel and they had the task of checking the potholes on the tarmac road, places where the Taliban might have placed mines. These poor guys were vulnerable to IEDs (Improvised Explosive Devices). These IEDs could explode when a member of the Taliban pressed a button on an electronic device. But in some places the Taliban laid simple anti-vehicle and anti-personnel mines. Just about half a kilometre from the Kandak, our de-mining team discovered there was a chance of an anti-vehicle mine in a pothole, and we stopped. The plan was to halt between 200–500m from the Lowa, to make sure that the area was clear of mines and Taliban. Then we went further and cleared the whole distance between the Kandak and the Lowa in order to transport the dead.

One soldier called Daud, from Faryab province, started to work on that hole and we kept watching the area around us. Gunfire was heard and at that moment we saw Daud falling on the ground. After the first shot, volleys of gunshots came from a ruined mosque in which Taliban were hiding and shooting at us. We all hid in a ditch on the side of the road and responded with our M4s. But we knew our efforts were useless. I suggested to Commander Andarabi that I and ten soldiers go towards the Kandak and from there we try to reach the back of the ruined mosque. He liked the idea and we started running in the ditch, our bodies bent over to make sure we were not seen and not hit. When I was sure that the Taliban could not see us and they were fully engaged in shooting towards Commander Andarabi's group, we got out of the ditch and jumped into a cornfield, where the enemy could not see us. From there we followed a path at right-angles to the road until I was sure we had gone far enough, and then I made another right-angled turn to the left. I was delighted to see a house right behind the ruined mosque. We asked the owner if we could use his house to attack the Taliban, and he did not object. From the roof of the house we could see four Taliban with their backs towards us, shooting at Commander Basir's group. I chose the three best snipers from those men who were with me and explained who was shooting which Talib. I would shoot one of them. The shooting must be carried out at exactly the same time so that the Taliban could not hide or escape. Three Taliban stopped moving after the shots, but one tried to hide. I did not give him that chance as my bullet reached his head. Silence. These Talibs were excellent shooters but not intelligent enough to realise we could approach them from a different direction. The Taliban used mosques to shoot at us frequently, knowing we were not permitted to shoot back because our government did not want to be seen as destroyers of mosques. The support of the local population was important but I wondered if the locals questioned this. If the Taliban were the defenders of Islam then why did they hide in mosques and make them targets?

We now had one more body to transport. Daud had been hit in the head and his helmet could not save him. But after that incident the rest of the journey was safe. When we reached the Lowa, we radioed our base to send a Chinook. Commander Andarabi was very happy with my plan and our achievement at the mosque. He reported that to the commander of our Kandak, who was in charge of 1,200 soldiers, and he made a note of my achievement in my file. Now that the area around Sangin Kandak was safe, helicopters were loaded with food to reach the Kandak.

After several days I was entitled to leave to see my family. My joining the army had a big impact on my relatives, especially my cousin, always admiring my commando clothes, putting his feet in my boots, saying, “Oh, too big for me.” He’d never been my play friend because of the age difference. I was five years older than him but, like an older brother, I always looked after him, taking his hand, helping him to walk far enough until he was tired. Then he asked me to carry him on my shoulders for the return home. He was scared of the dogs but felt safe with me. He always expressed his desire to join the ANA (Afghan National Army), but Uncle Baba Jan thought being in the army was not safe, especially fighting the cruellest enemy, the Taliban. However, my cousin Omid could not resist asking me one day, when we were eating fresh mulberries soaked in *kariz* water, "Amir could you please try to talk to my father?"

"About what?"

"About me getting married."

"Great, Omid, who is the girl?"

"Come on! There is no girl. She has not been born yet."

"Are you trying to tell me a stupid joke?"

"Yes, it sounds like a joke when I ask my father to let me join the army. So I thought you might be able to convince him. Tell him that not all the soldiers get killed."

"You're asking me to do something very difficult."

"Why?"

"What if something happens to you? Your father would blame me."

"Amir, please understand. My father has not been successful in providing for the family. We have hardly any land. Besides, I love the army and you are my hero."

"Ah, Omid, that is *reshwat-e lafzi*, bribing with words."

I did not ask Uncle Baba Jan immediately, but after several days I thought that life and death are in the hands of Allah. He saves lives in the battlefield and takes them away in the safest places.

Uncle Baba Jan loved me just like his son and always wanted to please me. When I told him about Omid's desire to join the army, for the first time he was prepared not to please me. But I kept insisting until he agreed. Beside Omid's desire to join the army, his service would change Uncle's life for the better, because Omid would be earning a salary while at home he was not working because jobs were not easily available. It had been a year since he graduated from high school and he was walking around without a job. Their land was so small that Uncle Baba Jan could manage it by himself.

Chapter 13

Sangin

In 2018, the first mass killing happened in Sangin district. We had a base for our Tolai consisting of sixty Afghan National Army soldiers and officers in the bazaar area to keep the residents and the bazaar safe. The Afghan government rented a *qila*, a fortress for these soldiers built with mud, but its walls were a metre thick. Since animosity and killing were part of the culture in this part of the country, Haji Lal Mohammad built this strong *qila* with watchtowers, ideal for the army and we thought it was the safest place. For five years, the Taliban tried to capture it, usually by hitting the gate of the *qila* with a truck full of explosives. But while they managed to destroy the gate, they could not go further because our snipers in the watchtowers shot them. But then Pakistan gave them a boring machine that could drill a tunnel big enough for a man to get through. With the help of GPS, they directed the excavation to reach under one of watchtowers and they had a large enough quantity of explosives strong enough to destroy a significant part of the fortress.

The Taliban had been working for months, and while the commander of the Tolai responsible for the safety of the fortress reported that there was some kind of noise coming from underground, the government ignored him, thinking nothing could happen from underground because the enemy was at least 500m away, hiding in ruins. This incident taught me how different we were. The Tajiks never built fortresses to protect themselves from their cousins and others. They were office workers or farmers, hoping for a safe and secure future for their children. But here fighting was like breathing, without it they could not survive and while they did not go to school, their minds were perfect for wars and battles. Otherwise, how could a simple person fight the might of NATO and a 380,000-strong well-trained Afghan National Army? The war was teaching me about my nation and its psychology.

We were given the mission to bring dead soldiers from this fortress, secure the road and areas around it, and capture our three posts, Kohsar1, Kohsar2 and Kohsar3, along the road between Lowa in Shoraba and Sangin districts. As the enemy was very strong, consisting of thousands, the commander of our Kandak sent sixty commandos and the commander of another Kandak based in Qandahar sent 100 commandos on a joint operation. The 100-strong army started their journey at 4 a.m. by armoured vehicle. But for the sixty of us, it was decided that we start our journey at 11 a.m., travelling by Chinook.

The plan was that after we reached our Kandak in Sangin, we would travel by armoured vehicles towards the posts captured by the Taliban while the other soldiers, travelling by road, inside twenty army tanks, would join us later. They also had two tanks filled with food and drink to bring for us.

After we landed in our Kandak in Sangin, we started travelling towards our posts. It was recorded that the Taliban had attacked these posts at least seventeen times. Each post had ten soldiers responsible for keeping the road safe. In Kohsar1 post, two soldiers were killed, in Kohsar2, four soldiers, but in Kohsar3, seven soldiers were killed and only three remained. After an intensive fight with the Taliban, who were equipped with heavy weapons inside our captured posts, we managed to take our posts back by killing all those Taliban inside. Fortunately, no one from our side was injured or killed.

After collecting the bodies, we continued to Sangin's bazaar, where one of our Tolais was based, in Haji Lal Mohammad's *qila*. During this expedition, we were attacked many times from a distance by Taliban snipers. But as we were inside the armoured vehicles, we were protected. There was the threat of a mass attack on our convoy too, but it did not happen.

When we reached the *qila*, to our horror we saw that a big part of it had been destroyed. We found two soldiers under the mud because it was rainy season and the rain in Sangin district was as heavy as a monsoon in India. Obviously, there were many bodies under the destroyed building, but it was impossible to reach them. Two soldiers were killed on a half-destroyed stairwell. The compound was the worst place. We encountered seventeen bodies and up to 2km away from the building we found the scattered bodies of the soldiers who had tried to escape but were targeted by Taliban waiting for them. The Taliban had binoculars to help them see at night. Out of sixty young soldiers and their officers, none was left alive.

The Taliban first detonated massive explosives, which they put at the end of their tunnel under the building. The explosion killed many soldiers who were asleep. The first watchtower was completely demolished by the explosion, killing the soldier posted there. Soldiers on top of the other tower, and in shock, were killed by snipers. In panic those soldiers still alive woke up and ran without knowing in what direction, and at that moment they were shot. So not a single person out of sixty was left alive. These young soldiers and officers were not infidels, as the Taliban claimed. They were Muslims who did not leave their *namaz* and had a mosque inside the *qila*. They were also the countrymen of the Taliban. The Taliban killed their own Muslim brothers.

The Taliban had been waiting for us to get inside the destroyed fortress and soon they surrounded us, firing from all directions. Commander Basir give me the task of making sure our soldiers were kept alive in the half-destroyed fortress, and he himself watched developments, giving orders. He was a fearless soldier, running from one corner to the other, encouraging our soldiers who were fighting an enemy at least ten times bigger in number. We had not eaten for the whole day because we were waiting for those 100 soldiers who were coming by road. Soldiers can fight without food but it is impossible without water. The wells inside the fortress had been destroyed by Taliban. News came that those 100 soldiers had to return to our Tolai in Sangin after they had been attacked by AF-10 Chinese missiles provided by Pakistan, resulting in the loss of seven commandos. Now we were fighting a cruel enemy without water and food. It was out of the question for a helicopter to come to that hell to bring us supplies. A helicopter could be shot down.

The night came and with it a miracle happened. Heavy rain poured from the sky and our soldiers opened their mouth towards the sky to drink each drop. I told those in safe areas to take their helmets off to collect water. A soldier found a pot and soon we quenched our thirst. The rain also had an impact on the enemy, making them stop shooting because they could not see anything. Our soldiers were able to look for food and fortunately manged to find a sack of rice and some pots. We boiled the rice using destroyed window frames as firewood, and without anything to add to it, started eating and prayed that the rain would not stop.

Commander Basir contacted our Lowa in Sangin and asked for help, but the commander of Lowa told him what happened to those 100 soldiers and said we had to find a way to get out of that hell by ourselves.

I was surprised to see such high morale among our commandos, despite not having proper food and facing a huge number of the enemy. We spent the night without losing a single soldier and the following day, when the rain stopped, faced continuous firing from the other side. By midnight, the rain came to the rescue again and that gave Commander Basir Andarabi the chance to have a chat with me.

"You know, Amir, help from our Lowa will not come," he said, offering me a cigarette.

"How many do you have?" I asked, smiling.

"What do you mean?"

"Cigarettes, commander."

"I am glad you have not lost your sense of humour, Amir."

"If I lose it, I lose the battle."

"Listen, if the rain continues like this until morning, we will get out of here. That is my plan."

"Isn't it better to wait?"

"Wait for what? To be killed? No one will come to rescue us."

I don't know if it was prayers from my mother that made the rain continue, but it did. We decided to leave the cursed compound now, having dead bodies to carry as well. The rain was so heavy that we could not see more than 2m in front, but our drivers met the challenge by ensuring their vehicles did not go off the road. The noisy rain also muffled the sound of the engines. Once we were at a distance of about 3km from the fortress, we were relatively safe. But it did not mean that the enemy was not along the road. However, if that were the case, they would not be there in big numbers.

We reached our Kandak outside Sangin Town but we were still far away from our Lowa where we'd started our journey two days before. Apart from bringing the dead to our Lowa in Shoraba, we also had the task of opening the road between our Kandak in Sangin and our Lowa in Shoraba, which meant clearing houses that the Taliban used to target our vehicles on the road. The sixty of us remaining were small in number to meet those challenges.

It was in 2016 that the Taliban created a special force called Red Unit. They already had another special force called Badri, created in 2011. These two units, highly trained in commando techniques, organised deadly attacks on the Afghan National Army. Apart from armoured vehicles and army tanks, they were equipped with the same weapons we were using, including Icom IC-V8 VHF radios, night vision equipment, heavy machine-guns and M4 carbines. How they received these weapons and training is beyond my comprehension. How is it possible that the US could not stop their training grounds in Pakistan and stop the weapons reaching them? Through all these years that we have been fighting the Taliban, the US government knew that the Taliban got their support from Pakistan. And yet, instead of punishing Pakistan, the US kept sending modern weapons. Obviously, some of these weapons were given to the Taliban.

In fact, the US was using its weapons against its own soldiers through Pakistan. Beside receiving arms, the enemy also received training from the Pakistani Army and experienced army officers from different countries who joined them. They also had teams of scientists and engineers from other countries. For the fundamentalist adventurer, there was only one place to carry out *jihad* in the name of Allah – Afghanistan.

The Kandak outside Sangin Town had been attacked many times, which resulted in the killing of our soldiers. Now the commander of our Lowa, realising the existence of the Kandak there was fruitless, decided to close this Kandak. But the transfer of 700 soldiers was not an easy task. Certainly not through the road network.

It was astonishing how we reached our Kandak compound without casualties while this one was surrounded. Obviously, the Taliban thought we were still in that half-destroyed fortress and they probably deployed all their forces to attack us there, hoping to kill another sixty soldiers.

Before midnight we heard an explosion coming from the direction of the fortress. The Taliban had filled a vehicle with explosives and a suicide driver had driven it inside the fortress. I assumed that the enemy was shocked to find out none of us was there and they had sent their suicide man to hell for nothing.

In our Kandak, we were relatively safe, but here also there was no food apart from flour, which we used to bake bread. At least we had something to eat after two days without food.

The commander of our Lowa radioed and asked us to locate houses that the Taliban used to attack us.

We did that and soon US Army planes started bombing these houses. But Commander Andarabi was not satisfied, knowing the enemy were still hiding in those houses, pretending they were simple village people.

"We must get rid of these people once and for all," Commander Andarabi said while we were strolling in the morning. We used the morning walk to discuss our next mission and what to do.

"What do you suggest?" I asked, offering him a packet of cigarettes from my pocket for him to take one.

"After the American bombing, we search the houses around the Kandak."

"But what if the Taliban respond and we end up killing and injuring innocent people?"

"By now the innocent people know that these houses are not safe and have gone. Anyway, we do not have any alternative. We have come here for this task and I do not want it half-finished."

Out of sixty commandos, Andarabi chose twenty-five and briefed them about the operation. He suggested we enter houses not destroyed by US bombing and search for the enemy. This had to happen in darkness and we had to move in complete silence to ensure the enemy did not notice what was going on. He chose a cloudy night when the sky was dark. We left the base just before midnight. I was ordered to walk at least 100m ahead of our single-file company. Obviously, my task was more dangerous than others but Andarabi believed I had enough experience and ability to be safe. Walking slowly and in absolute silence, I reached the first house and waited there for the rest of the group to join me. Andarabi walked by, placing himself in the middle.

The strong walnut wood door had a chain behind it to keep it shut. Andarabi ordered one soldier to climb on the shoulder of another to reach the top of the courtyard wall and from there he jumped inside and opened the door for us. We rushed inside the single-storey building.

Once we were sure that no one was near enough to the Kandak to attack a helicopter, we radioed back to our Lowa and a Chinook landed, bringing thirty US Marines. Obviously, they realised how bad our situation was. Apart from this helicopter, two more landed, bringing food. The same helicopters took the dead to our Lowa base in Shoraba. The US Marines risked their own lives to help us. Chinooks could easily be targeted. One had already been destroyed, killing all marines on board some years earlier. I was ashamed because my own people were killing us and foreign soldiers who were there to protect us.

One thing I learned from the Americans was how to relax even when a terrible war was going on. I do not know how they found out that we loved wrestling. Tall marines challenged our soldiers to wrestling and our soldiers responded. The wrestling was still going on when they started playing volleyball with us. I also joined in. The commander of this Kandak told us that his soldier had not played volleyball for a long time, since the attacks intensified. While we did fine in wrestling, we were hopeless at volleyball against men who were 2m tall.

If we thought our mission was over we were wrong. Now the mission designed to be for forty-eight hours was extended for nineteen days and during this time the US Marines stayed with us. We had the task of ensuring the Kandak was safe. But the commander of our Lowa knew that the safety of the Kandak would be short and still had a plan to relocate our soldiers from there. After nineteen days we left by Chinook on the same day that 140 soldiers from Kabul arrived to support the Kandak.

Because of the hard work and intensity of the fights that the commandos were involved in, we had three cycles:

1. Three months Yellow Cycle to fight the enemy for different periods of time
2. Red Cycle to have a break
3. Green Cycle, ready to be deployed if needed but at the same time carry on with further training

After the dreadful fight in Sangin, which we barely managed to survive, we waited for our commander to let us go for our Red Cycle, to have a break and to visit our families. We were thankful to god that none of us had been killed in the last mission. But the commander of Qol-e Urdo, a man in charge of 30,000 soldiers and officers, had contacted the commander of our Kandak at the exact time we were preparing ourselves for our break. And we had to conduct a new mission near another of our bases at Sabit Qadam.

Sabit Qadam base consisted of a Kandak of 700 soldiers and officers. Its location was not far from two villages from where the Taliban were using long-range weapons to attack the camp, which resulted in frequent casualties. As with the operation we had just finished, the US could not bombard these two villages because of the fear of killing innocent people. So it was decided that forty-eight commandos, including Basir Andarabi and me, accompany thirty US Marines travelling by three Chinook helicopters. These helicopters would land away from the villages, to avoid being hit by the long-range weapons the Taliban possessed. But knowing the Taliban used landmines, we also took landmine engineers with us who were experts in using landmine detectors. They became so experienced that they could immediately recognise that there was a landmine when they heard certain sounds from their detectors.

We organised ourselves into four groups. The Americans would be in touch with us from a distance and support us if a big danger threatened us. No one knew the strength of the enemy. The second group in which Basir Andarabi was the leader also had the same role as the US Marines. Andarabi would wait at the bottom of a hill with fifteen soldiers. The remaining soldiers were divided between Commander Homaion and me, responsible for searching houses.

There were two villages located at the bottom of a green hill, just in front of a fast-flowing river. Each village had between ten to twelve houses and one mosque, which they all shared. We knew that some of these houses and the mosque were used by Taliban who attacked Sabit Qadam base.

When the helicopters landed, it was around 2 a.m. The sky was clear and full of bright stars, the moon in half. To make sure that the enemy did not have time to escape, we surrounded the villages and immediately started searching houses. My group found some Kalashnikovs and three long-range weapons, and Commander Homaion reported by radio that he'd also found weapons and three suspected Taliban. We informed Andarabi that we had found suspected Taliban with weapons. Thinking we were in a place where many different weapons could be found, Andarabi radioed us that he would also join us with his group. I joked that he wanted to be killed and he replied in that case he preferred not to leave us alone if there was a threat of death. We did not suspect that things would turn nasty in these villages and we thought these suspected Taliban may not be Taliban because everyone carried weapons in this part of Afghanistan.

Houses were scattered around these two villages and we did not risk walking from one house to another without having the de-mining engineer in front of the rest of us following his footsteps in single-file. Just about half an hour after Basir Andarabi had been in touch, he radioed to tell us, with pain in his voice, that he and some soldiers in his group had been injured by a mine explosion. I wanted to find out more but our communication stopped. Thinking he might have been badly injured or even killed, I sent some of my soldiers to where Andarabi and his soldiers were. My group also carried stretchers. I instructed the de-mining engineer to go quickly with four of my soldiers, but to be careful.

I carried out my mission quickly, but whenever I radioed Homaion, I did not receive a reply. This had a psychological impact on me, thinking he might have been injured too. When I finished my village, I radioed the de-mining engineer to come back to me to take our group to Andarabi. When I reached Andarabi, I was delighted to see he was standing on his feet. But his face was covered in blood, and blood was pouring from around his right eye.

Apparently, they had approached a courtyard that had three walls intact but one wall demolished. There was a tarpaulin sheet across this space, designed to look as if it had been placed there for privacy. But by now we had become experts in knowing the Taliban's tricks, because they also hid long-range weapons under solar panels. The first person who approached the tarpaulin was the de-mining engineer. But as soon as he tried to remove it, there was an explosion and he was injured. A soldier rushed to pick him up from the ground, but another explosion made him fall on the landmine. The mine had cut his body in two. The Taliban indeed had a long-range weapon under the tarpaulin sheet but they only kept one side of the sheet without mines for them to reach the weapon. The way that they'd planted the mines was the work of evil experts, killing three soldiers and injuring four others. To make sure we did not lose the injured soldiers I ordered our safe soldiers to carry the dead and injured to helicopters where the Americans were waiting for us. Fortunately, Homaion also appeared without any injuries in his group. It was around four in the morning when we left the cursed place.

My hope of taking leave to see my family before I'd seen any casualties vanished. Those soldiers were closer to me than my brother, because they were prepared to lose their lives to protect me and I would have done the same for them. The bond between soldiers fighting a cruel enemy is much stronger than family ties.

When I reached our base with our captured enemies, our soldiers started attacking them after hearing what happened to our soldiers and how many were dead and wounded. I tried my best to keep them away, but there were more than 100 soldiers. Impossible to control. Not finding any way to disperse them, I took a hose pipe and turned the fast flowing water on our soldiers. Finally, they got the message and left the prisoners. But when I looked at them they were half dead. Unlike the Taliban, who beat our soldiers after capturing them and then shooting them, we followed international law, keeping the prisoners safe. The Taliban had the audacity to film themselves torturing and shooting our soldiers, then posted the videos on social media.

Soon Captain Karim appeared to talk with me. He was independent of all army organisations, responsible for the investigation of conduct.

"I cannot send these prisoners to our Qol-e Urdo," he said waving his right hand towards the prisoners lying on the ground, faces covered with blood.

"But why, Captain Karim?"

"If they die, I will be responsible."

"They are not going to die."

“How can you guarantee that? And why were the soldiers allowed to do this?”

“We lost our brothers at Sabit Qadam. The enemy mined the area in such a clever way that even for our mine engineer it was impossible to detect. These guys you worry about could have told us of the danger. Instead they wanted us to be killed.”

“But we are different, Captain Amir. Tell me why soldiers were allowed to do this?”

“Are you accusing me? I did not order our soldiers to beat these bastards.”

“Perhaps soldiers do not follow your instructions.”

“Listen, Karim! I just returned from one of those terrible operations, not sleeping all night, and now you want to interrogate me?”

“We have to follow army rules.”

I turned my back on Captain Karim and walked towards my room to get some sleep. But sleep did not come.

I ordered my soldiers to provide water and food for the prisoners and keep them in a room where they could sleep and rest. But if I thought it was the last time Captain Karim was going to interrogate me, I was wrong. The following day, when I was still physically and emotionally tired, Karim came to me, this time with a file, and put a piece of paper in front of me, full of questions for me to answer. I read the questions, some of them were strong accusations. The worst thing that can happen to a soldier is when his own brother in arm stands against him. I thought about my ambition. I wanted to be a senior officer. But these questions, if not designed to dismiss me from the army, would go on my file, which would damage my career. Negative thoughts came to my mind, the thought of disappointment on the face of Jamila first and then disappointment on the face of my father. What can a trained soldier do when he loses his job? In my case it would be back to farming with my father. Even if that was an option, I was the lucky one because we had land and Father had become an expert in the farming business. But it was unfair what Karim was doing to me. Of course he was following the rules. But still these rules made me angry because the enemy did not follow any rules. We'd lost three soldiers and had four seriously injured. To me it seemed that Karim was not concerned about them. I'd told my soldiers many times that we do not kill our war prisoners, not like the Taliban, because they were not our teachers. But how could I control the emotions of our soldiers when we brought the prisoners back? And because I could not control them, Karim was accusing me of not being a capable commander. All these issues made me angry and without being able to stop myself, I tore up the piece of paper and walked out.

I could see the shock and astonishment on Karim's face before I left. Finally, the commander of our Kandak, Commander Yusof, a man in charge of 700 soldiers, interfered and told Karim to back off.

Chapter 14

Kabul – A Different Battle

In December 2018, Asadullah Khalid became defence minister and the first thing he did was rotate army personnel, especially those like us in a hot spot like Helmand, a place where we had paid a heavy price with our lives, sustaining injuries and death. He was a well-experienced soldier himself, although he had not attended an army academy. He learned the art of battle in fighting the Taliban as a guerrilla leader when the Taliban were in power after the fall of the Mujahideen in 1996. After the fall of the Taliban, he became the head of the National Directorate of Security. The CIA and the Americans liked him because he recovered stingers that had been given to the Mujahideen to fight the USSR, and there was a chance that these weapons would fall into the hands of al-Qaeda to be used against US planes. He was a bright young man and President Ghani preferred to have young men in his cabinet rather than old men, who might have lots of experience but were not willing to adapt and learn.

His decision to rotate the army made him popular among army personnel. They felt as though the new minister cared about their wellbeing. He had been the target of three assassination attempts, two of which resulted in minor injuries and one a major injury that required treatment in the US. On Khalid's return from America, President Ghani appointed him as minister of defence, hoping that he would be able to defeat the Taliban.

It was a hard and confusing time for the Afghan government and the army. President Trump was now in power and the US recognised the Taliban. They were not regarded as a terrorist group anymore. They were now regarded as political opposition against the Afghan government, their opposition expressed by armed struggle. The US decided to negotiate peace with the Taliban to stop them fighting the Afghan government and instead participate in a national election to see if they had enough support to form the next government. The Taliban demanded that the Afghan government, which was democratically elected, resign before the election.

Without a government in power, the Afghan Army would have no direction and the Taliban would use this time to capture the whole of Afghanistan. Now they were known to be liars and their empty guarantees were not to be trusted. But the Taliban were proving they weren't just a fighting force. They were also making gains on the political map, becoming a known opposition to the Afghan government and even having the audacity to make the ruling government the third party in negotiating the peace process.

So it seemed only two relevant groups were there to negotiate peace: the US and the Taliban. The Taliban's ultimate demand was that US troops leave immediately and the Afghan government resigned.

After three years serving in the army in Helmand, I was posted to Kabul. Although I was out of danger, physical exhaustion was replaced by mental exhaustion, because when there was an operation going on for a long time and it continued the whole night, I had to be in my office, receiving information about our forces and passing it to the secretarial teams of the senior generals, who advised what was to be done. Some incidents were not a priority and so the secretaries, themselves experienced army men, filtered the information and sent on only the details of those incidents that deserved attention.

For me, sleep deprivation wasn't a big problem. But whenever my brothers in arms were in danger, that had a psychological impact on me, especially in cases when they were surrounded by the enemy and it was impossible either for help to reach them, or it would reach them very late. The enemy was improving in all different aspects of war with the best training and acquiring the latest weapons. And because the government was corrupt, the Taliban recruited many young people, including underage boys, those who suffered from extreme poverty. When soldiers in great danger contacted me and asked for help, sometimes

I felt powerless and wanted to be with them, fighting the enemy. I had been in their situation many times and I knew how desperate it was.

The Taliban did not respect any rules, including Islamic rules that forbade attacking Muslims in the month of Ramadan or during Eid celebrations. We celebrated Eid but I was still on duty when I was contacted by a post in Ajirestan district in Ghazni province. In Ajirestan we had sixty commandos and more than 250 Afghan National Army and police, all there to defend this district against the Taliban. Two commandos were patrolling the bazaar when they were attacked and shot dead. The commander of the Kandak based in Ajirestan ordered some of his soldiers to go into the bazaar and bring back the bodies of the two soldiers. The enemy had already planned a bigger attack using the incident as a diversion. A truck full of explosives driven by a suicide driver hit the outer wall of the compound and within minutes Taliban poured from all different directions, getting inside the compound through the gap created by the suicide driver. They opened fire on anything that moved in front of them. The deputy of the Tolai was killed during the surprise attack. In the panic, those still alive ran away, but they managed to group together and proceeded towards a nearby hill, aiming to attack the compound that was now in the hands of the Taliban. But they were ambushed and most of them killed. Out of 310 soldiers, only sixteen commandos managed to escape, walking for eighteen hours to reach a village from where they reported their location to me. I asked for a helicopter dispatch and the commandos were rescued.

The Taliban not only captured Ajirestan district but, encouraged by their first major victory, attacked Ghazni province. To our surprise, I received a message that Ghazni had fallen into the hands of the Taliban. After three days of hard battle, the whole of Ghazni, including Ajirestan, was liberated. But when the army compound was taken back, our soldiers found that the bodies of all those soldiers killed were either burned or disfigured by acid. Identification was impossible.

The Afghan Army had a policy to immediately inform families about the fate of dead soldiers, but in this case had no clue which body was supposed to be given to which family. So it was decided that all these soldiers would be buried respectfully in one mass grave and all families could attend. The government also had a policy to give money to the families of the deceased. One of the dead was assumed to be an army doctor, but we didn't know five of our comrades, including the doctor, were taken prisoner.

The doctor was forced to treat the injured Taliban. After four months, he was asked to treat a Taliban commander. The commander showed kindness and allowed him to contact his family to inform them he was alive. It took more than a year for the doctor to escape and report to the army again. He shocked his family when one day he entered his house to see his wife was still mourning his loss.

It was my responsibility to know what was going on throughout the whole of Ghazni province. I became an expert with computer, phone and radio reporting, but the fear was suffocating. I was terrified of failing my comrades and not being able to help them.

Knowing we needed the help of the local community, we recruited some of the locals, who spied on the Taliban for us, giving us information about the Taliban's plans. We found a mullah in the Zana Khan district of Ghazni who could provide information in exchange for money. We all knew that mullahs were always willing to do anything for money, because they received very little financial support from the community. Mullah Shahbaz was one of these. To prove he was giving us a good service, Mullah Shahbaz informed us that an important Taliban commander had decided to invite many Taliban for lunch after Friday prayers.

Our Kandak in Ghazni province prepared itself for attacking the Taliban during lunch. To speed things up, four government 777 model helicopters with forty soldiers in each flew to where the lunch was supposed to be. But as soon as our soldiers landed, they found themselves surrounded by Taliban. There were three times more Talban than there were soldiers. Realising the lunch was a trap, they fought their way back to the helicopters, but only twenty-six soldiers managed to escape. Taliban spies had managed to find out about Mullah Shahbaz. We discovered that, subsequently, Mullah Shahbaz was brutally killed in public to show that if anyone spied for the government, they would share the same fate.

Chapter 15

In Kabul

Women were the biggest winners in society when the Taliban lost power. And women were not content will simply being teachers, office workers, engineers or even doctors. They wanted to change Afghanistan and for that reason some of them became members of the Afghan parliament. Encouraged by their success, two women stood for the office of president, and frankly they were strong candidates. Their action showed that our nation was changing, tolerating and trusting a woman to be the next leader of the country.

Those women who went to Iran with their families to escape the civil war during the reign of the Mujahideen and the Taliban were better educated because they were graduates of Iranian universities. Besides good qualifications, the language they used was superior, using expanded vocabulary that those who had stayed in Afghanistan could not use. No matter how some people tried to say our education wasn't bad during Taliban rule and under the Mujahideen, the truth was that most of these women were self-taught or received their education in a secret environment. Not the best for high academical achievement.

The returnees learned art and literature from Iranian women and soon we had women appearing on television as newsreaders and managing feature programmes. They also published books in Afghanistan and sent them to international competitions, mainly in Iran, surprising the people in both Iran and Afghanistan by winning prizes. Women's power made some men jealous and there was a sad tragedy when an emerging young poet was murdered by her husband for the crime of writing romantic poetry. But she was completely innocent and did not have a muse. Even if she had a muse, she did not deserve to be killed.

No women appeared wearing miniskirts, as had happened before the Mujahideen and the Taliban, but they'd become very fashionable, even more so than the Iranian women who they followed in almost all aspects of their lives. While in Iran, women walking in the streets wore big grey or black coats, the Afghan women in Kabul wore trousers, long skirts and sometimes traditional Afghan dress, modified and modernised. These fashionable women never wore the burqa, and did not cover their heads with scarves as Iranian women did. Texting with smartphones became part of their lives and those texts were not only for their female friends. Girls texted boys and sometimes they met each other. While sex before marriage was forbidden, young people satisfied themselves in other ways. Of course, none of these things would have happened if the parents did not tolerate what the young people did.

In Kabul, Hashmat from Logar province, a native Pashto speaker who spoke Persian just like me, became a good friend. He was a commando too and lived with his wife and 6-year-old twin boys, Nabil and Shaker. When we had a free day, which was usually Fridays, unless an important mission was going on, we went to Paghman Valley just outside Kabul with our families. It was cool in the summer. We shared the cost of the taxi but Jamila and I paid for the food, which was normally a kebab with good *Shomali* salad. Jamila also prepared *doogh*, a cool drink made of sour yoghurt, water and fresh mint. Hashmat paid for the local spirit, not as good as whisky but cheap and it had the effect we wanted. We drank, laughed, watched the children play, and the women gossiped while they prepared. Because of the effect of the alcohol, very little food was left when it was time to leave. What there was we shared with birds, ducks and stray cats.

We spread a *qalin* – a handmade rug – under the shade of a walnut tree. The women prepared salad first for the drinkers, and for themselves brewed green tea and ate *noqul* with it, which is a sugar-coated almond. After lunch Hashmat took his *tanboor*, an Afghan string instrument similar to a guitar, and started playing. He was an excellent musician and had a melodious voice. One day he sang a song that made Jamila cry:

Each day before I go to war
I think of you
Remembering how we ran in green fields.
Sometimes when the enemy fires
I see your eyes and forget the danger.
But when I get killed
Will you bury me?
Will you remember me?

Seeing the impact of the song on Jamila, I asked Hashmat never again to bring the sadness of war home to destroy a day of happiness.

The Taliban were not in power but their influence in rural areas of Afghanistan remained. What I described was the life of women in major cities such as Kabul, Mazar-e Sharif, Herat, Panjshir and Badakhshan, not cities such as Qandahar and Helmand, strongholds of the Taliban, where women experienced little freedom. In these places people believed that everything was in the hand of god. Hospitals were not needed because prayers from the Quran could cure the most dangerous illnesses. In such an environment, mullahs were well-respected and they had the life of men who had wealth without a day's work. But what happened to some unfortunate women did not happen in Qandahar or Helmand. It happened in Kunduz, among those people who had migrated from Helmand about a century ago.

Here a mullah by the name of Mullah Landay emerged. Landay means short in Pashto and people believed that he could cure all illnesses with the power of his breath, reciting the Quran. But beside all his curing power he was also able to make woman have children, and this was very important in our country. Men wanted their name to be carried after their death and a woman without a child was worthless. Those who were rich married again but those who did not have money searched for a holy man like Mullah Landay. In our society men do not think that not having a child may be related to them, they always blame the women. Mullah Landay, the man who could make women pregnant through prayer, became famous and women either sold their jewellery or borrowed money to visit him. This rich mullah had his own followers and servants to clean and cook for him. But then videos emerged of the mullah having sex with women while reciting words from the Quran.

Mullah Landay persuaded a policewoman to spread the word about his spiritual power to the women who did not have children. Under her influence women went to see him. During their first visit, the mullah recited from the Quran, wrote words from the Quran, and asked the women to wear the paper these words were written on as a charm around their neck after covering it in leather or cloth. But of course none of these words worked, especially coming from a cheating mullah. Then the mullah proposed the women have sex with him and because his body was a holy body, mixing it with the body of the woman would enable the woman to have a child. At this point some women stopped seeing him, but those under a lot of pressure, including those beaten by their husbands, agreed. In the mullah's bedroom, the mullah had sex with these women but the women were unaware that the policewoman was hiding and recording the act on a mobile phone. It was shocking to see some women really enjoyed having sex with the mullah because they did not have a loving husband. Some women had a child after having sex with Mullah Landay.

The mullah threatened the women that if they did not bring him money regularly he would send the videos to their husbands. You can imagine what these women would face. Ultimate death.

While the mullah was very clever, he was not careful. And one day, when he left his mobile phone unattended, a person who suspected his activities looked at his video files and was shocked by what he saw. The man wanted to expose the mullah and he immediately circulated the videos through social media, unaware of the impact on the unfortunate women. Not only were these women killed, but the husbands killed the children too. It was obvious the policewoman, herself married, was also the lover of the mullah. But she was fortunate enough to be caught by the police and put in prison. As for the mullah, he vanished. I guess since he was an expert in criminal activities, he ran away from Kunduz, got rid of his turban and long beard, wore Western clothes and started living in another province. Afghanistan is a big country and his crime was not a big priority in a country where a war was going on and young soldiers lost their lives every day.

After two decades of a stagnating economy, there was healthy economic growth. A property boom was one of the major influences. Afghan people from Europe and America came back to Afghanistan to invest in property. They increased the price of property beyond limit. The powerful men and warlords grabbed the most valuable public lands and built palaces, exploiting the government's weakness and corruption. Some of these land-grabbers were senior government officials like those who were ministers. Their palaces had large swimming pools, saunas and Jacuzzis, and the windows of the houses were bulletproof. One with vulgar taste made the architect design a huge eagle on his flat rooftop as big as a small aeroplane. One can imagine that the cost of building such an eagle was the equivalent of an entire flat for an ordinary person.

One day I was walking on the streets of Wazir Akbar Khan, one of the most affluent places, where Europeans and Americans lived before the war. The houses were built with very good taste and were just as beautiful as houses in the US with manicured lawns, and big cypress and willow trees. One street was blocked by armed men who, though not working for the government, had erected a checkpoint. They stopped me from going further and said that the whole street had been bought by Defence Minister Fahim. Minister Fahim, who had been a guerrilla fighter in the past with no money, now had the whole street for himself in the most expensive part of Kabul. That was not the only place owned by him. Just outside Kabul he'd built a huge house surrounded by land. In this land were orchards, vineyards and he kept tigers in cages. The other penniless warlord was the owner of the whole city of Mazar-e Sharif. Atta Mohammad Noor, now the governor of Mazar-e Sharif, had his own airstrip and had enough money to buy properties in the west. His son studied at Sandhurst – the top military training academy in the UK, his fees paid by his father. He collected tax from people in Mazar-e Sharif and put it in his pocket. The government did not dare to question it because he had his own strong private army. While the rich became richer and some who had been penniless became multi-millionaires, the general poor stayed poor. Their poverty was exploited even by those returning to Afghanistan. Sixty-year-old men married 20-year-old girls or younger, their houses full of cheap servants who were paid between $100 to $200 per month.

It was not only that the warlords made the existence of the government weak but the government itself was divided. After the election, Abdullah Abdullah, who had won the first round of the election, did not accept Ashraf Ghani as president. For some months the government did not function well and the previous president, Karzai, continued to govern, until the US sent Senator Kerry to mediate between the two. After days of negotiation, Abdullah and Ghani decided to work together. Ghani became president and Abdullah became chief executive, but none obeyed the other. Abdullah appointed his own men in very important posts and Ghani did the same, putting his own men in charge.

Before the Taliban came to power in 1996, they promised that they would stop the Mujahideen killing innocent people. That is how they attracted support, because on almost every street in Kabul was a checkpoint, making the life of citizens difficult. During the rule of the Mujahideen, Kabulis could not go out of the house to buy food. And if they left their houses, they risked their lives. Sometimes the Mujahideen practised target-shooting from their base on the mountains by killing innocent people who walked about in the city.

Life did not have any value to them, but that was nothing compared to shooting rockets from the top of the mountain, aiming to hit their enemies but missing their target, the rockets landing on the houses of ordinary people, killing families, wiping them out.

As the Taliban were unable to defeat the Afghan Army in the battlefield, they created a special suicide force with the task of blowing themselves up in crowded areas, killing as many people as they could. The purpose for such barbarianism was to show the world that the Afghan government was incapable of providing security for its people.

The Taliban also tried to create tension between communities by exploiting differences in ethnicity and religion. They sent small boys wearing jackets full of explosives into Takia Khana and mosques of the Shias sect and by doing so, they managed to kill hundreds of people in big gatherings. Those who survived the suicide bombs were targeted by the Taliban with Kalashnikovs in hand. Photos emerged of these sites showing carpets, walls and ceilings painted with blood.

Sometimes the Taliban killed people in busy markets, regardless of differences in religion or ethnicity. One incident really affected me. I knew four brothers. They had no father and by trying very hard, saving their money, they managed to open a second-hand shop at the heart of the old city. A suicide bomber blew himself up just outside their shop and killed all four brothers, making their mother childless.

If people were fortunate enough to survive the Taliban, they could not escape the criminals. Nowhere in the country was safe at night, including Kabul. Sometimes gangsters wore army and police uniforms, entering houses owned by rich people and taking valuables such as jewellery and money. They targeted the banks even during the day, stopping bulletproof vans, killing the drivers and the guards and taking all the money. Another crime on the rise was kidnapping rich people. Businessmen or their children were kidnapped and ransoms demanded. When the police interfered, the kidnappers killed their victims.

Not many people were unaffected by the killing during this war against the Taliban and by the criminals. Even my Uncle Baba Jan was not left alone. He had some land with an excellent view ideal for building a hotel where the tourists from Kabul could stay. Someone from a faraway village who was a commander during the rule of the Mujahideen and still had his armed men was interested in buying this land and building a hotel. Wars made him rich and greedy. One day he approached Baba Jan and asked him to sell that particular land to him. But Baba Jan, despite needing money, did not want a ruthless Mujahideen commander to be close to him, and didn't want a hotel built on the land either. But this rejection came with a heavy price. When my cousin Omid was visiting his parents during a break from the army, he was lured to a quiet place and shot to death, his body riddled with bullets. Uncle Baba Jan had no enemy that he suspected of murdering his son. He was a peaceful person, but the killing of his son caused such a shock that he had a heart attack. Uncle Baba Jan was sure he knew who'd killed his son, but there was no witness and no evidence against the Mujahideen commander. And even if there had been, the corrupt government wasn't going to do anything, fearing the Mujahideen commander would take arms against them.

The killing of Omid had a big impact on me and for more than a year I planned my revenge. I'm glad I didn't do anything because I would have put my own family in danger, including my parents. The Mujahideen commander had four strong, grown-up sons, all busy in banditry, just like their father. For them, killing innocent people was just like drinking water. Omid was a cousin that I loved like a brother, because I did not have a brother and I looked after him when he was a baby. He always followed me, not only physically walking behind but also mentally, and that is why he joined the army. Uncle Baba Jan was worried about his safety in the army but he was not aware that he would be killed not far from his home in a safe country. Fortunately, my depression at Omid's killing reduced as time went on, but whenever I went to Nijrab and faced Uncle Baba Jan, the memory of Omid came to me. I could see him on his father's shoulders when he was just a small boy and I was jumping behind Uncle Baba Jan to let me carry Omid on my own shoulders. The other sad thing was that he was engaged to a beautiful girl from our village and was supposed to get married. His future in-laws and fiancée were very proud of him, knowing he was a brave commando with the prospect of becoming a senior officer in due course.

I was reading Hafiz's poetry one evening after dinner when Hashmat came to see me.

"Do you want to go to our usual place?"

"You mean to smoke *chillum*?"

"Yes, in our *chaykhana*."

"I like the *chillum* place."

In our language we call shisha *chillum*. Now in Kabul there were many cafés that served Italian coffee or chai, Tajikistan style where customers sat on a *takht* – wooden platform. Over the *takht* handmade rugs were laid and there were cushions over the carpet to lie on, just like those miniatures of Omar Khayyam in which beautiful *saqi* poured wine into his cup. But here in these *chaykhanas* there was no wine. To be honest, tea with that *chillum* tasted better than wine and talks with Hashmat were a good replacement for poetry. I wondered how a man with such knowledge in history decided to become an army officer. When I asked him, he said, "Teaching in school is also a fight against ignorance but right now I must fight the ignorant who want to close schools." Before joining the army, he was a history teacher in Habibia High School, one of the best schools in Kabul. The way he told me about history was better than watching a movie. All the characters came to life with his words.

When we sat on a *takht* in Rumi Chaykhana, I said, "Tell me about Mir Masjidi."

"You like Mir Masjidi because he was from your area and your father's name is Masjidi too."

Mir Masjidi was a freedom fighter who fought against the British when they invaded our country between 1838–1842. Unable to defeat him on the battlefield, the British managed to poison him with the help of one his followers, in exchange for money. It was true that my grandfather named my father Masjidi after that great freedom fighter.

"Actually I came here to tell you about something else."

"What? Tell me."

"Wait my friend, not before tea and *chillum*."

It was a beautiful evening. The sky was filled with bright stars and the full moon was shining. While the streets of Kabul was full of noise during the day because of the cars, here at about 10 p.m. the garden of the Rumi Chaykhana was quiet. People talked in whispers so as not to disturb the peace of the night. There were young men and young girls and they seldom spoke, instead holding hands, smiling, gazing into each other's eyes.

"Youth," Hashmat said, pointing with his chin towards a young couple.

"You are not a grandma yourself, Hashmat."

"Grandma, ha?"

"You sound like one when you're in this mood."

"I am not in a good mood."

"Tell me what bothers you?"

"I knew a boy from my village in Logar. His mother died when he was only 6 years old but his father, because of poverty, could not marry again. Most days his father was out looking for a job to feed himself and his son. The son was alone and one day he disappeared. We thought at the beginning that he must have been attacked by an animal or he was drowned in the fast running Logar River. But none of us thought that he could have been kidnapped. You know in our country the shameful *bacha bāzī* is very common, in which a terrible person kidnaps a small boy and makes him dance for an audience to make money out of him, and at the end of performance someone rich gives money to the kidnapper to have sex with the boy.

"Yesterday my neighbour told me about a Logari boy who would perform in Istalif and I want to rescue this boy because my gut says he is the same boy from my village who disappeared."

"Wow, man. Facing a dangerous gangster and you know he will not be alone. Besides how do you know if he is the same boy?"

"I am not scared of a gangster and even if this boy is not the same, at least I may manage to make the life of a boy safe in my country."

"You know I cannot allow you to do this alone."

"I don't want you to put your life in danger because of my madness."

"You are not mad, Hashmat. What you are doing we must all do."

"It is tomorrow evening."

"I'll wait for you at home. Now, let's smoke our *chillum*."

At around 8 p.m. the next evening, Hashmat came to my house with Raziq, an Afghan National Army officer whom I knew and who was a distant relative of Hashmat. We all picked up our pistols, which we were allowed to carry from our posts for our safety. My only hope was that Hashmat had a plan, one that wasn't just jumping into action.

Seeing that they were wearing hunters' waistcoats, I wore the same because these waistcoats had big inside pockets in which we could hide our pistols.

What Hashmat told me brought back old memories of the time when I was learning the Quran from our mullah in our village and saw the abuse of that small orphan boy, Hafiz. I was glad that I was brave enough to tell my father what happened. My action could have easily made the villagers stand against my father, but that did not happen. Of course, I could not stop the mullah completely and he was probably now somewhere in another village doing the same. But at least my village was safe.

Hashmat had hired a car and on the way, in order to relax, he started singing. I loved his voice and when he stopped, Raziq cracked jokes. He was a funny man. Jamila was not aware of what I was doing that night because I had told her that I was going to a wedding with my friend Hashmat. Part of the story was true. Where we were going was a wedding party and the main attraction for this party was the boy who was dancing. The people who organised the wedding had also invited some excellent musicians from Kahrabat to accompany the boy.

Takht-e Istalif is a well-known place in Afghanistan, popular in the summer when people from all over the country enjoy the beauty. The *takht* was a plateau above the hill. It was mentioned for the first time in a memoir by Babur, the King of Kabul, who used to go there in the summer and drink wine, about 600 years ago. In those days Istalif produced its own red and white wine, but Babur admired the white wine. Obviously, Islam in those days had not penetrated the soul of the people in Istalif and they continued to produce their wine. When the communists took over in 1978, Istalif again became a place for drinking. But this time the communists brought their Russian Vodka. Since the Mujahideen took over, there were no vodka parties in Istalif, and when the Taliban came to power, even picnics happened less often.

The Taliban did not want people to enjoy life. They converted cinema halls to mosques and destroyed beautiful parks to build big mosques in their place. The money came from Arab sheiks who themselves went to Thailand to enjoy nature and women. During the reign of the Mujahideen, the ugly *bacha bāzī* flourished and people hoped that the Taliban would put an end to it but the Taliban only focused on curtailing the freedom of women and ignored what was happening to boys who were abused. In fact, since the Taliban stayed away from the women, they themselves abused boys who joined them. These boys were from the poorest families and the families hoped that by letting them join the Taliban, at least they would have a place to sleep and food to eat. So madrasas became the centre of abuse. Taliban mullahs especially abused those boys who were extremely shy and could not stop their advances. Even if a boy was not shy, he could not report what happened to him because of society and shame. Normally the society judged that if the boy complained it meant the boy himself was to blame. The face the ordinary people saw was the face of enlightened and god-fearing man.

Because of his voice, Hashmat had been invited by someone he knew. We were guests of honour since Hashmat was going to sing for free and he was allowed to bring as many friends as he wanted. Obviously, the professional musicians from Kharabat were taking a good amount of money. This was the wedding of a rich man's son. Handmade rugs and cushions were placed to create a square at the centre for the dancer. First tea with sweets and sweetmeats were served. The fresh air was now mixed with smoke from *chillum*, cigarettes and hashish. Hashmat, Raziq and I indulged in smoking *chillum* but refrained from hashish. We never liked it and knew the effect of that crazy plant on the brain.

First Nawayee, the famous singer, started singing while playing harmonium as well, accompanied by *tanboor*, *rabab* and *tabla* players. He was well received for his singing skills. Then a female dancer from the same Kharabat started dancing, but she was not beautiful. She had a slim body, a flat chest, and wore heavy makeup to conceal her age. She failed to draw much attention from the audience.

At least ten teenagers appeared with *aftaba-lagan* and soap to wash the men's hands prior to eating. One thing I loved was our custom of washing hands before and after food and was I was surprised when foreign soldiers ate with us and tried to imitate our way of eating with their fingers, but never bothered to wash their hands. Some rubbed their greasy fingers against their army uniforms.

The food was magnificent. There was lamb kebab – I estimated at least three big lambs were slaughtered – *badenjan borani*, *aashak*, *mantoo*, spinach, *kofteh* and delightful *qabili palau*, without which no wedding is complete. During the dinner the groom appeared to greet every individual and encouraged us to eat and drink as much as we could. He also joined us in eating, sitting in the most prominent position.

"God, he can't even be 16 years old." Hashmat pointed towards the bridegroom with his chin.

"Now you can imagine the age of the bride – anything between 9 and 15," Raziq said, picking up a big chunk of *mantoo*, mixing it with mincemeat and chickpea on the platter. Food was shared on a big platter.

"The real entertainment is going to start after the dinner when the boy starts to dance." Hashmat smiled.

"Perhaps he is waiting for you to start singing after dinner. I didn't know you liked boys," I said.

"Shut up, I am here to stop this ugly culture," he whispered to prevent others hearing him. Most of the guests were there to watch the boy dancing.

"Don't get excited. I'm just joking."

"You two come with me after dinner. I have to tell you something."

I watched people eating and whenever there was a platter half empty someone rushed to fill it. Guests wore their most beautiful clothes. Lines of electric bulbs on wires above us gave off different colours. Guests laughed at each other's jokes, enjoying the food and drink. But no alcohol was served and yet I knew there must be a secret gathering somewhere where guests had alcoholic drinks. As part of respect for elders and religious people, no one drank in public. As for us, I knew we had to stay sober if we wanted to get out alive. Some guests came with their pistols and even AK47s just to show off. But it wasn't necessary for protection. After the Russian invasion, men's jewellery was weapon enough, something I hated.

After dinner, once again *aftaba-lagan* was brought for the guests to wash their hands and then tea was served with sweets.

"It is time for us to have privacy." Hashmat stood up and began to walk. Raziq and I followed.

"I have a plan," Hashmat said, lighting a cigarette and offering one to Raziq and me.

"I am glad you have one," I said sarcastically.

"They will request that I sing soon. I'll make sure that the hosts enjoy it. After me the singing and dancing will go on until an hour or two before sunrise. At that moment I tell the man who is in charge of the boy that I would like to spend a little time in private with the boy. Of course he'll think I would like to have sex with the boy and he will get some money from me for this. The host always provides a spare room. When I am inside the room, the man who is holding the boy will wait for the boy to come out of the room. At that moment you guys must hit the man on the head, so he is unconscious, and then we all escape together."

"What happens if there is more than one man behind the door and if some other guests who want to have sex with the boy are waiting in the corridor?"

"Pray there is none, but if it is too complicated, we do not complete the mission and will do it another time."

People loved what Hashmat sung and of course the same boy was brought to dance while he was singing. Understanding the situation, Hashmat sung some fast songs and then slow songs to make the boy move fast and slow, intoxicating the guests. Hashmat kept singing until there was a need for a break and it was at that time that Hashmat made his move, having a conversation in whispers with the man who was handling the boy. We saw the three of them, the boy, Hashmat and the handler, leave the party. We followed, but the handler, who was walking in front, was guiding Hashmat and the boy towards the cornfield to have complete privacy, instead of going to the house, because there were guests everywhere.

"Raziq, we are in luck, my friend," I said

"I can't believe it."

These men protected their boys even more than their own wives and family. The dancing boys brought enormous joy and pleasure to them while their wives were only to look after the children and the house. They loved these boys, who were a source of income – sometimes considerable income depending on how beautiful and graceful they were. The man with the boy employed some bodyguards to protect the boy and I could see two men with handguns on their belts who always stayed close.

Fear strangled my heart. There was no way to avoid casualties. Either we had to kill them, or they would kill us. The worst thing would be that we would be remembered with shame that we were killed during the kidnapping of a boy dancer because we wanted him for ourselves.

With his singing, Hashmat won the heart of the boy's owner. Professional singers were harmless, not like gangsters trying to kidnap a boy. Most of these singers were of loose character, trying to take advantage of the boy with no courage or ability to steal him. So when Hashmat walked away with the owner of the boy and the boy himself, I was shocked and relieved at the same time.

These dancing boys have always been abused through history, but wars made the situation even worse. The Taliban built *madrasas* for boys to learn the Quran and for them to stay there overnight. Poor parents who could not afford to feed them sent their boys to these *madrasas*, where the boys were abused, especially at night by their own teachers. When the story leaked out, the Taliban leadership covered them and protected the teachers, who were fighting men too. To them these fighting men were more important than a boy. I only heard about this because a boy told his story to a major newspaper without being identified. He could only tell his story when he managed to run away from the *madrasa*. Taliban who claimed to follow Islam strictly could not resist committing this sin against humanity.

When the three of them were far from the wedding, Hashmat and the boy disappeared in the field. I had been following them, under the cover of the night's darkness. The handler had squatted, waiting for the two of them to emerge. While we were hiding in the cornfield and slowly making our way to the handler without making any noise, I began to fear that the man might be armed. I had already picked up a big rock after Hashmat told me about his plan. We approached the man from behind and when he was about to look back I hit him on the head, knocking him unconscious, hoping he wasn't dead. We whispered Hashmat's name and walked quickly towards our car with him and the boy.

Chapter 16

The Last Stand, Saluting our Flag

Seven months before the fall of the government I was posted to Farah province, one of the biggest provinces bordering Iran. Here I was promoted to the rank of colonel and I commanded a unit of Kandak comprising 800 soldiers. By now, neighbouring provinces were losing their districts and the enemy was advancing. But Farah province was different because of the skills and bravery of Brigadier Roheed Paikar, Chief of Pillars of Lowa. Here we became close friends because he made clear plans and carried them out. As the war progressed, one province after another fell into the hands of the Taliban, such as Qandahar, Badghis, Zabul and Ghazni. But we held Farah province and continued fighting against the Taliban in the city and districts. Only fifteen days before, Ashraf Ghani left the country, while both Brigadier Roheed and I fought in the city, the commander of our Lowa, General Nabi Ahmadzai, radioed and urged us to leave the city and help defend the Lowa.

The enemy surrounded our compound in an open space ideal for the planes to attack them. In the past they never dared to attack a Lowa if the Lowa was on top of a hill or in the middle of the desert because, firstly, the compound would be defended, causing them to sustain huge casualties, and there was also air support for our forces. With air support, the Taliban would have been sitting ducks. In the past their favourite tactics were road ambushes and hiding among civilians in cities. But now, after we lost US air support, we were very vulnerable.

By now we had heard that Deputy Governor Zakir had already surrendered to the Taliban while he was in the city, but the governor, along with some other high officials, were in Lowa's compound waiting to negotiate their surrender, basically asking them for forgiveness and to allow them to live. This term was not acceptable for Brigadier Roheed, Sakhi, or me. We were encouraged to see the support of our soldiers who preferred an honourable death to the humiliation of surrender, and we knew there was no guarantee that the Taliban would be true to their word. Many times before they had asked our units to surrender, saying that their safety was guaranteed. But as soon as they surrendered, the Taliban killed them.

After many days of intense fighting, suffering casualties due to rockets fired over short distances, Roheed received another message from the Taliban. These messages came in on a daily basis, but this one had a strong commitment from the Taliban commander that the life of our soldiers would be safe if we surrender. Roheed, Sakhi and I held a meeting.

"There is no way we can defeat them," I said, looking around Roheed's office, which was like a bunker with sandbags, where we had our meeting.

"But they cannot take this compound from us either," Roheed said.

"Maybe not by fighting. But we are slowly running out of ammunition and food, and these things by themselves will result in defeat," Sakhi said.

"But I hope we will get support from other bases just like before." Roheed looked into my eyes, asking me to confirm this.

"With respect, sir, it is not the same as before. Perhaps only five or six provinces are still free and they are fighting for their own survival, in need of help," I said.

"So what do you suggest?" Roheed asked.

"I don't know. You make a decision."

We talked as though we were all sharing a nightmare on a dark night. None of us was able to wake up or wake the others. How was it possible that such a big army could crumble so fast and provinces taken by the Taliban, one after another? Perhaps it was Taliban propaganda. Afghan radios did not confirm their advancement, so maybe they were using this technique against us, convincing us that we did not have any support and must surrender. Was it possible we were going to be fooled by a trick? Maybe it was only Farah province that was captured. If we surrendered, we would be ashamed of what we had done because others were fighting.

The office, without any decoration or a painting on the walls, seemed an odd place to be in. Normally we were in the field fighting and used our offices seldom. We also had bedrooms in our compound for us, but we used them not more than ten nights through the years. We fought in the field and when we returned to our compound, we either left the same day for our break or spent a single night, maximum. Our beds were sitting in the tanks, army vehicles, or sleeping mountains and deserts.

A soldier entered the room and, after saluting, asked for Commander Roheed to go to the commander of the Lowa's office.

"Sakhi, you and Amir also come with me," Commander Roheed said after placing his hat.

"But sir, he asked only for you," I said.

"Yes. But it is time that you both be present and decide what you want to do after our meeting."

It didn't sound good and I guessed there might be disagreement and Commander Roheed did not want to be alone. He was giving us a choice of sides.

I entered the office of General Ahmadzai, the commander of the Lowa, after Roheed and immediately recognised the governor of Farah province sitting next to the most senior judge. Other seats were taken by high officials who, like the governor and the judge, ran away from the city and had come to our compound for their safety. With Commander Roheed in front of us we saluted together.

"Commander Roheed, we have no choice but to surrender. The whole compound is surrounded by Taliban."

"Sorry, sir. But I cannot accept," Roheed said firmly.

"What are you talking about?" General Ahmadzai said, eyes almost popping out of their sockets, in clear shock. "The Taliban have agreed to let us go if we agreed to surrender."

"Sir, in the past they have done the same. But after surrender, those soldiers who agreed were killed. The three of us with my soldiers under my command only survived because we never agreed to surrender."

"This is outrageous and unbelievable."

"I am sorry, sir."

"But this is mutiny."

"I wouldn't call it that, sir."

"Soldier, I order you."

At that moment Roheed took his hand gun out and raised his voice. "I will shoot anyone who wants to surrender."

"Are you mad?"

"Sir, I prefer to die instead of being captured."

"You do this alone?"

"No, sir. I ask all our soldiers and officers to choose for themselves."

"But you are risking the lives of more than three thousand people."

"I give them the choice."

"I must answer to the Taliban to protect lives."

"I will answer you, sir, in an hour's time."

With that last sentence, Commander Roheed left the room and we followed. We went back to his office. I took a packet of cigarettes out of my pocket and offered one for each.

"It is a tough one, Commander," I said, lighting my cigarette.

"What do you mean a tough one?" Commander Roheed asked, looking into my eyes. "We have been in this situation many times."

"Yes, but in those situations it was you who made the decision. Right now you are acting against the most senior officer, risking the lives of three thousand personnel. If we lose and are captured it will be you responsible."

"You mean I am alone in this?"

"No, Commander we are with you," Sakhi chimed in.

"These people have never seen the front line. They stayed in their air-conditioned offices, ordering us around while we spent nights next to dead and injured soldiers. We fought and never surrendered for two reasons. Because we are not cowards and because the enemy has never been honest. A shameful surrender is worse than being killed. You, Amir, go and gather all the soldiers, officers and civilians here. I will ask them what they want to do. If they want to surrender, then we have no choice. But I will tell you one thing. The enemy knows you two and me, and they will never let us live."

"I saw General Ahmadzai already redecorated his office," Sakhi said laughing.

"What?"

"You guys did not notice?"

"Notice what?"

"He has taken down the big framed photo of President Ghani from behind his desk."

"Sakhi, I don't see anything these days, apart from my anger," Roheed said.

I went out and asked all our soldiers, officers and civilians to come to Commander Roheed's office. Commander Roheed addressed them, clearly told them the situation, and asked what they wanted. It was there that I realised Roheed was more respected than the commander of the Lowa. They all assured him that they preferred to die fighting. Commander Roheed did not talk for long. After his speech he asked me to go to General Ahmadzai's office to tell him he should contact the Taliban and ask them to give us until 7 p.m., when Roheed would give them his answer. The commander of the Lowa agreed.

"Now, you two, organise the whole camp for an escape." Commander Roheed said when I came back. "Don't worry. I am not mad, thinking of storming the main gate, where we will all be slaughtered. One of you go to Rahim, the man in charge of the bulldozer, and tell him to make a hole in the far end of the compound wall at 6:45 p.m. But before that, all useful items should be put in army vehicles and army tanks. Our personnel must gather their personal belongings too. The whole operation must be dealt with in an orderly fashion. We have thirty army tanks that scare the Taliban. Immediately after the opening, one tank in which you, Amir, sit, will be parked facing right. You, Sakhi, your tank will be parked to the left. The guns must be pointed to the left and right. When the Taliban appear there, and there will not be a large number because they will be mostly in front of the gate, you both fire nonstop. Obviously, they will run away, but they will attack again, sending fighters from the front of the gate. I will be in the first army tank. Between army vehicles you must station one army tank accordingly and spread them evenly, because they will protect the line. We travel single-file. You two keep firing until all of our soldiers and civilians are out inside the tanks and vehicles. At the end, you will follow."

Sakhi and I did what Commander Roheed ordered. The whole operation was carried out with good discipline, but my heart was beating fast. What if we failed and risked the lives of so many men? I kept going from one corner to the other, sometimes even joking to a soldier to keep the morale high.

Our soldiers did not have many belongings. I filled three tanks with water, as Commander Roheed had asked me to do. Our journey would be through the Bagwa Desert, one of the biggest deserts in Afghanistan. Army tanks were filled with food, but we knew that food and water would not last long. It was quite possible that we could escape the Taliban, but die in the desert. Roheed's destination was the Iranian border.

"What do we do in this vast desert once we get out?" I asked Roheed.

"We continue our escape until we reach another army unit. On the way, we contact others. There must be others who are still fighting, and if that is the case we will join them."

"But we haven't had any contact from anyone for days," Sakhi said.

"We must keep our hope alive. As I said, we have been in this situation many times before," Roheed said.

"I agree. We wait until 6:45 p.m. Rahim will be the first man in action," Sakhi said.

Time sped by. I worried we may not be prepared on time because we'd never faced such a situation. But to my surprise, an hour before our escape time, all soldiers and civilians were ready. Army tanks and vehicles stood in one line, ready to be turned on by their drivers. At exactly 6:45 p.m., Rahim hit the wall with his bulldozer and in only ten minutes he had created the opening we wanted. He pushed the debris away so our vehicles would get out easily. Standing on the tower of my tank, I saluted our flag for the last time, knowing it would be replaced by the Taliban flag. That white flag seemed the darkest flag to me, a flag against all values I had. At 6:55 p.m., my tank stood on the right and Sakhi's tank to the left, guns pointing. Roheed's tank rushed outside and was the first. Behind it followed army vehicles carrying our personnel, and then tanks at intervals. But about ten minutes later, the Taliban appeared from right and left. I started firing nonstop, and so did Sakhi. Our action pushed the Taliban away but they very quickly regrouped and stacked the middle of our caravan with heavy guns on top of their pickup trucks. Our tanks in the middle responded, and once again Taliban fighters disappeared, only to appear again in even larger numbers. I could see the dust, the smoke, and the destroyed Taliban pickup trucks.

Commander Roheed was in the first vehicle. We travelled single-file. Our speed was based on the speed of army tanks. Roheed, with the help of GPS, was navigating. Farah province is very hot in July and August, but the desert is twice as hot. If we got lost, there would be no chance of surviving, but by now we'd become experts in navigation. We tried to contact other bases and units, but had no luck, and we worried that they had all been captured by the Taliban. The unbearable heat made everyone thirsty, but strict rationing was followed and no one was allowed more water than his provision. Fortunately, we were all healthy and no one was injured when the Taliban attacked us during our escape.

We stopped travelling at midnight. Some people slept in the vehicles and others slept out in the open. By now the desert was cooler and there was a mild breeze. The sky was full of stars and the half-moon gave the impression that everything was calm and peaceful. The enemy was celebrating its victory and did not care to capture 2,000 hopeless people in the middle of the desert. The Taliban now ruled our country. They had all army bases and provinces under their control and were busy looting.

Amidst the timeless dunes, where whispered secrets of aeons past intertwined with the arid breeze, a vast canvas of sands stretched to embrace the horizon's tender touch. Sun-soaked silence reigned, broken only by the rhythmic dance of grains and the ethereal symphony of solitude's expanse, and the desert's heart beat with the pulse of timeless beauty.

The desert lay in front of us like a vast sea – just as frightening as the sea with unexpected turns and storms. My father had told me many times how caravans disappeared in the Bagwa Desert, and now we were travelling in the same desert. All hopes were based on Commander Roheed and my intelligence and ability. Like Roheed, I could navigate with the help of the stars, but he was much better at it than me. We had DAGR GPS, used by the US Army, but even with that sometimes army units travelling in the Bagwa Desert were lost. But in the past there was air support and a lost unit could easily be guided and supported from the air. Now we were on our own within the limitless body of the desert. Sometimes the wild wind pushed the brown sand onto the windscreens of our vehicles causing it to stick there, almost impossible to move, making it difficult for our drivers to see what was ahead.

On the second day, the driver of the vehicle in which Commander Roheed was travelling misjudged the depth of soft sand on the ground and instead of reversing tried to go forward. But that made the vehicle wheels sink deeper into the sand, and soon the wheels stopped turning. I was in the second vehicle and I told my driver to stop. I walked over to Roheed and we discussed how to get the vehicle out. This wasn't something new to us because we'd had the same experiences in the past, once in the middle of the night.

Without further delay I asked our soldiers to tie a rope to the back of the stuck vehicle and fasten the other end to an army tank. The operation was successful, but now the first vehicle had to change course, avoiding the soft sand, going much slower. The other vehicles followed the path created by the tyres of the first vehicle.

If we thought that was our only problem that day we were wrong. In the late afternoon the wind became very strong, making it difficult to see anything in front of us, at times not even a metre ahead, because the wind pushed huge amounts of sand onto the windscreen. But Commander Roheed did not stop and, now crawling, we followed, hoping none of our vehicles would get lost. Commander Roheed hoped that the wind would pass after an hour or so, but then he radioed me.

"We must stop, Amir."

"You're right, we will lose each other."

"Send a message to all vehicles that we stop here. We need to make sure that we keep checking that the wheels don't get stuck – that wind is blowing the sand so much there's a danger of that happening. If it does happen, then we need to move the vehicle about five metres forward and then back again to free it."

"Yes, Commander."

I sent a message to make sure that all vehicles heard what Commander Roheed instructed, and they all responded that they had heard. I got out of the vehicle, moving quickly to avoid sand getting inside, but the sand blinded me. It took some time to open my eyes to see if our wheels were buried but, fortunately, that was not the case. The sand travelled yet further, carried by the wind. That meant the other vehicles were also safe. Once back in my vehicle, I radioed the others and told them that if they left their own vehicles to check the wheels, they should cover their eyes with a cloth and move really quickly. They should also keep their back to the wind.

At the Iranian border, we saw guards on watchtowers and the whole border was fenced to prevent Afghans crossing. Forty years of war had resulted in a huge influx of refugees escaping war only to face inhumane treatment by both their Pakistani and Iranian neighbours. There were countless killings by police and soldiers and the rape of women and children, some as young as 10 years old. But when a government is involved in a savage war and it tries to survive, defending the right of its nation is not a priority and, in any case, when Afghanistan was safe and there was no war, no one wanted to leave his country to go to these countries to be treated badly. In fact many people from Iran and Pakistan returned to Afghanistan to rebuild houses destroyed by war after the fall of the Taliban in 2001. In 2001, Kabul looked like Berlin after the Second World War. But within fifteen years it was transformed by the people themselves while the government lacked the ability to provide infrastructure.

Commander Roheed ordered his driver to stop at least 500m away from the fence. The guards kept looking towards us through their binoculars and we knew they were nervous. Commander Roheed tried to contact the guards using his mobile, but was unsuccessful. Whatever sign we made, the Iranians did not respond and we assumed that was because they did not have the authority to engage in communication. We were angry because we had with us men who had been dead for four days, and two critically injured soldiers who needed assistance. Besides that, we had not eaten for four days and we were running out of drinking water. When night came, we continued sending signals with torches and vehicle lights, but still they did not respond.

About 10 a.m. the following day, their Jeep approached the fence and gave a signal. Commander Roheed and I went to talk to two men who got out of the Jeep.

"I am Brigadier Roheed. Taliban have attacked our base in Farah and they also captured neighbouring provinces. We tried to contact our other units but they have not responded and I feel they've fallen into the hands of the Taliban."

"Sorry to hear that, sir. I am Lieutenant Danish, responsible for border security. How can I help you, Brigadier?"

"Can you provide us with some accommodation? We have four dead men and two injured. We want the dead men to be buried honourably and the injured treated."

For a considerable time the lieutenant kept quiet. Then he said, "I must contact our superiors, sir."

Hours passed and we started to get worried. What would happen if the Iranians rejected us? Where could we go from here? Obviously, we risked the life of civilians. A soldier is prepared to die and it is part of his life. He is responsible for the defence of others and if he cannot defend, then he is prepared to die. Of course, there is the option to surrender, but we had already rejected that. These hours were the most anxious and longest hours of our lives. The three of us, Roheed, Sakhi and I, kept looking at each other. But we could not utter a word in case what we said became reality. And what else could we say apart from that we had gambled with the lives of civilians?

We'd almost finished our drinking water and it was becoming a possibility that even if we had managed to survive the enemy by some miracle, we would not survive the thirst in this hot desert when the temperature rose up to 52°C. In the late afternoon, Lieutenant Danish came to the fence and waved towards us. I must say that I panicked more then than when I faced the enemy's bullet, fearing rejection.

"My government has agreed to allow you to enter our soil." Danish scanned the parked vehicles.

"We thank you, officer, but will you give us a document stating you received our weapons, army tanks and army vehicles?" Commander Roheed spoke bravely, knowing it was a hopeless situation.

"Well, Brigadier, I did not discuss that with my superiors."

"Please, sir, go back and ask them."

Danish walked slowly to his vehicle. We guessed they would keep us for there for some time until we agreed to what they wanted – they would give us safe passage in return for whatever we had. But to our surprise he came back an hour later and said that his senior officers had agreed.

They provided water and food for our tired and hungry caravan. Buses came and transported us to the border town of Zabul. After three days we heard the good news that they would fly us to Kabul.

Since there were many people with us, the transportation continued over several hours. Commander Roheed, Sakhi and I took the fourteenth flight, but there were going to be at least two more flights. The reason we could not take the last flight was because we got a message from our army base in Kabul that the Taliban were approaching the city and we were required there urgently. But when we reached Kabul Airport, we heard the sad news that on that exact day our president had left Afghanistan and now the whole country was in the hands of the Taliban. Only Kabul Airport was guarded by our army, the British and the Americans. They advised us not to leave, but Commander Roheed did not agree and we could not leave him alone. The Taliban kept sending messages to the Afghan Army still at the airport to come out unarmed and no one would be harmed. Commander Roheed decided to take the risk.

We came out with our uniforms on and were relieved that the Taliban were true to their word, at least this time. Without having any contact with them or any other person, the first thing we did was go to a *hammam* to wash ourselves after days of not being able to. The Iranians had provided drinking water and food for us, but no washing facilities. The hot water took the pain of tiredness away and we were happy that we were clean. But the sadness we felt at the fact that Afghanistan was in the hands of the Taliban could not be washed from our skins. Once again, our leaders had failed us and made sure they could all leave Afghanistan safely, including the defence minister and the other ministers. Fortunately, Sakhi had an apartment in Kabul and he suggested we stay with him until we decided what to do next.

We spent four days in Sakhi's apartment discussing what to do and finally we all decided to go to Panjshir. When the Afghan government collapsed, many army officers and soldiers gathered around Ahmad Masoud, the son of Ahmad Shah Masoud, who was one of the greatest resistance fighters who finally defeated the Soviet Union. His son was now the leader of new resistance fighters, determined to fight against the Taliban. Wearing civilian clothes we paid 10,000 Afghani and took a bus to Panjshir where, to our surprise, apart from a normal check that no one was carrying weapons, all passengers were allowed to reach their destinations.

When we reached Panjshir, seeing many army officers and soldiers around Masoud we were confident we could put up a good fight and our goal was to keep Panjshir out of the control of the

Taliban. The local people, who worshiped Ahmad Shah Masoud – the father of Ahmad Masoud – were all determined to fight until their last drop of blood. The appearance of officers and soldiers and the local enthusiasm affected us too, but whenever we tried to have an audience with Ahmad Masoud, we were told he was very busy. And they were right because we could see that people from all around the country had gathered in Panjshir.

Three days passed. We slept in the open air, bought our own food from shops, and waited patiently. But when we met Ahmad Masoud, he was indifferent towards us and we felt that he mainly relied on his own people from Panjshir. His father had done the same at the beginning when he started fighting the Soviet Union, but very soon he realised that he could not fight the Soviet Union without countrywide support. However, we concluded that young Ahmad Masoud was not like his father and, apart from a degree from a military academy in England, he had no experience of fighting the enemy. Disappointed that our experience and ability were ignored, we decided to leave Panjshir.

We returned to Kabul and after five days in Sakhi's apartment, he suggested we all go to Iran, because his brother had a house there and we all could live there until we found jobs, which, like many Afghan refugees, would probably be labourers' jobs. We had no problem with doing manual work. That was far better than walking the streets of our own country in the hands of the Taliban.

To make sure we were not recognised, we decided that we would go separately, taking different buses to Herat and from there to Iran. By now the Taliban showed no mercy when they captured army officers of the old regime. Their forgiveness was short-lived and we heard stories of politicians and army officers either killed on the spot or sent to prison never to be released. The first person to leave Kabul was Commander Roheed. After him Sakhi went the following day, and I was the last person to leave. During my time in Kabul, I contacted Siraj, a distant relative who I trusted, and I used his mobile to phone Jamila every day to see how she was. She told me that the Taliban checked our apartment every day and night and I must not go to see her. Being so near and yet not able to see her saddened me. The emotional impact was much more difficult than facing the enemy's bullet. I missed Jamila, whom I loved very much. I could only see her when I was allowed to go home. But now, even that was impossible. In my heart I welcomed the idea of going to Iran because then I would be able to send for Jamila. My father was an old man and he could easily accompany her.

After I finished my conversation with Jamila, Siraj's telephone rang. Each time his phone rang I panicked, and yet I knew if the Taliban were informed that I was there in that apartment, they would not phone Siraj to say they were coming for me. I checked the number and it was Roheed's.

"I have very bad news, Amir," he said.

"Go on then, why do you hesitate,' I bellowed. "Tell me what happened."

"They killed Sakhi."

"What?"

Roheed said Sakhi was travelling in a taxi by himself but when the taxi driver stopped for petrol, Sakhi left the taxi to buy a bottle of water. At exactly that moment a group of Taliban heading to Panjshir appeared from nowhere, travelling in high speed pickups. They also stopped for petrol. Their commander, who was from the same village as Sakhi, recognised him and killed him on the spot, not just because he'd fought the Taliban for many years but because he'd had a feud with him and his family for a long time.

Stunned by what I heard, I could not believe it. Sakhi, a young man proud of his fitness and a fearless fighter against the Taliban, was alive just the day before, and after hugging me with a smile he had said, "See you on the other side." Now the other side was not just Iran.

"How do you know all these things?"

"The Taliban contacted his family and they phoned his brother in Iran. His brother phoned me to warn me what happened."

We were going to Iran because Sakhi's brother was there. But now we had to change our plan. Roheed came back to Kabul and this time we rented a room in a cheap hotel. In disguise, I managed to go to the house of another distant relative to borrow some money to pay for rent and food.

One evening my phone rang and I was surprised to hear the voice of Brigadier Basir Andarabi. He was in India for eye treatment. During fighting against the Taliban, shrapnel had entered his left eye. He was taken to Delhi where doctors operated. They managed to save his life but he lost his left eye. I put the phone on speaker for Roheed to hear and he told us that General Yasin Zia, our head of armed forces, was now in London trying to get financial and political support for fighting against the Taliban. Basir said that General Akmal Amir and some other officers would soon create a group and he would be a member of that group. He also wanted us to join, to which we agreed. We would be operating in Salang.

The Hindu Kush Mountains are the highest in our country. They are branches of the Himalia Mountains. Always covered by white snow, the icecaps are a source of water for many rivers. Until the day we made this mountain our home from where to attack the Taliban, Hindu Kush for me was a place of magnificent beauty. Many times I came to Salang, in the foothills, in the summer, for picnics with my friends. We ate peaches and mulberries, and listened to the sound of the river. Where we had our picnics was all green and a little higher everything was covered with snow. Houses were built with stone and wood. Sometimes we dared to get into the river, but as soon as the water reached our knees we rushed back to dry land. We never dared to camp there at night knowing how cold it could be, and this place was at the bottom of the mountain with the temperature of -15°C in January. But the higher parts would reach the minimum temperature of between -40°C to -50°C. I assumed where we were had a temperature of -20°C, and it was December. All around us was covered with white snow and sometimes the snow continued for days. But when it was sunny we noticed the glory of this beautiful mountain. The sun melted the snow and water trickled in small streams. Delighted by this phenomenon, I would stretch out on my stomach, drinking water, which made the others laugh. The sun's generosity extended beyond providing water because only under its warmth could we sleep. Every person had a plastic sheet to cover himself when it snowed and he kept that cover over himself at night. We did not have a tent. Because of the cold we did not sleep at night – we slept in the day when it was sunny. Sometimes we did not sleep for three to four days and nights waiting for the sun to come out.

When I was younger, in the summer we slept on the flat roof but before falling asleep I watched the mountain. My father said that this mountain was a home for snow leopards, wolves and other wild animals. The mountain under the moonlight seemed magnificent and mysterious. Now I wondered what was hiding in the mountain that had become a shelter for me. It is possible that the wolves and the leopards were looking for prey. The mountain with its high strong sides, its valleys and depths, its valleys full of water in the summer, was a source of water for the rivers. It was also a place where you had to be careful. If you took a wrong step you could fall to your death. Its layers were like the pages of book with stories of history, a book millions of years old. Night shaded a different colour on the mountain, dark black, dark blue and dark grey. The deep snow covered the dangerous falls but if you were tricked, you would meet your death.

It was sunny and from where I was sitting I could clearly see the town of Charikar, the road zig-zagging through the mountain, cars and lorries speeding towards their destination.

"What are you dreaming about, Amir?" General Akmal Ameer walked towards me and looked around, seeing the vast landscape of the mountain, the town of Charikar, the road.

"It is as though there is no war, it's so peaceful," I said.

"I wish it was true."

"If only we were allowed to enjoy peace."

"Listen, Amir, I've received a message that there is food waiting down there. I'm going with some others to fetch it. There is the possibility of an attack while a convoy of Taliban move on the road. You stay here and look after our belongings."

"Okay, General."

"Call me Akmal. There is no general here. We are all equal."

In a way I was happy that the others had gone, leaving me in that peaceful solitude. Not willing to show weakness by admitting that any one of us missed his family, we never talked about our parents, children and wives. But in my mind I always had a conversation with Jamila. I remembered occasions that always stayed in my mind. The way she wiped sweat from my forehead when it was a hot summer, looking into my eyes while I was eating her delicious cooking, smiling. She paused, watching me while I was eating, enjoying that gaze more than enjoying her food. The day she presented me a magnificent *khamak doozi piraan wa tonbaan* when I returned home after four months' absence. Different moments came to my mind as if my mind had become a cinema screen.

I was in deep thought and by now my friends had been gone for more than an hour. I heard a sound. I looked around but there was nobody. Thinking I'd made a mistake, once again I continued with my dreams. But then a stone fell from the top of the cliff. I jumped up and picked up my gun, thinking the enemy had waited somewhere nearby until my friends had gone and then could attack me. I looked towards the top of the cliff and there it was, a grey wolf. His sparkling, almond-shaped eyes were focused on me. I guessed he was hungry and had smelled the food we had. For a while he kept looking at me and I looked at him, and then I looked for some food for him. All I could find was some bread and a can of sardines. I threw the food up to him and watched him coming down, picking up the bread and the sardines and quickly disappearing. I realised how hungry he must have been to eat bread.

When the others returned I told them that I'd seen a wolf. An elderly person who'd volunteered to be with us fighting the Taliban said, "Yes, I saw wolf's paw prints in the snow."

"The loneliness in the mountains has affected your brain, my friend." Basir Andarabi laughed, and the others did the same, even the elderly person, making sure he was not left out.

"Trust me, I gave him a can of sardines and some bread."

"Amir, it's okay if you ate the sardines, no one is criticising you, even if we are short on supplies," Akmal Ameer said, and he smiled as he put his hand on my left shoulder.

"No, believe me."

"This is the first time I've heard of a wolf eating bread," Salim from Salang said.

There was no way for me to prove I'd seen a wolf, so I kept quiet. But the following day at exactly the same time, the wolf appeared. This time Roheed saw him first. The wolf came closer. When the others moved their hands or made a gesture, the wolf opened its mouth, showing its teeth, making threatening noises, but when I got near it, it calmed down.

"Don't go near, Amir!" someone shouted.

"Please, one of you go and get a can of sardines and some bread," I shouted back, looking at the wolf. There was a kind of gentleness and nobility in it.

"You know we struggle with supplies," said Jmal, who was known for his jokes.

"It is okay, I'll feed him my share."

I named my wolf Gurg. When I was a child I heard horrible stories of packs of wolves attacking villagers, giving me the impression that this animal was cruel. But this one was not threatening me and I could see kindness in his eyes, something like friendship. Of course, my friends never cut my share. At first they complained, but after a while they gave up.

The beauty of Gurg lay in his wild and majestic presence. The sleek, powerful body adorned by shades of grey. His eyes, often a piercing amber or deep golden hue, held an enigmatic intelligence and an air of mystery.

The wolf moved with grace and agility, muscles ripping beneath his fur a testament of a beautiful body. His pointed ears and keen sense of smell and hearing added to the allure of apex predator. His howl was haunting and melodic, a symbol of wilderness.

Here I was taking refuge in this mountain running away from my own countrymen, the Taliban, finding a kind wolf who offers friendship. There was more humanity in this wolf than the Taliban.

My friendship with Gurg was a unique and extraordinary bond that transcended the boundaries of species. It was built on trust, mutual respect, and shared experiences. We communicated through gestures, body language, and a deep understanding of each other's needs. We supported and protected each other, forging a connection that's both primal and profound. Gurg circled around me at night to protect me and I protected him from being harmed by my group, who all carried guns and thought that wolves were our enemies because they all had stories how wolves killed their animals. Our friendship served as a testament to the power of empathy and companionship across the animal kingdom. I was prepared to share my ration with Gurg and that was not easy when I was suffering from hunger. Because of the continuous wars in my country, I knew that even children carried guns and shot wild animals. I wanted to teach my people that without wolves our nature would not be complete. I wanted to come to this mountain after the war to spend some time with Gurg.

Officer Haroon and I slept under a cliff for protection against the wind, but we could never sleep at night because of the cold. Beside the cold, Haroon could not close his eyes for a minute, worrying that the wolf might attack, because we could see his eyes while he was circling around the two of us the whole night. I knew he was there to show his friendship to me. Otherwise he could go to the others and attack them. We always slept in pairs, next to each other.

The cold was unbearable and because of that we could not sleep now even during the day. For a soldier, sleep is very important because sleep and food give him strength. We were able to eat enough not to feel hungry, but we could not avoid the cold, which robbed us of sleep. General Akmal Ameer, Brigadier Basir Andarabi and Brigadier Roheed decided that if we stayed there, chances were we would die of the cold. So they said we should move to lower ground and search for an *aghail*, where shepherds keep their sheep during warm weather. The day we were packing, I kept looking for my friend Gurg, to see if he would come to say goodbye. Unfortunately, there was no sign of him. I could not shout his name in case my voice echoed round the mountain and the enemy became aware of our presence. Disappointed, I took the rear of the line and from time to time looked back, hoping to see Gurg.

When we had moved quite a distance, I saw Gurg running towards us, not from behind but from our right-hand side. When he was about 100m away, he walked alongside, sometimes lifting his head to see me and communicating with his eyes. The others said that my friend was very loyal but I did not pay attention to their conversation. I was making conversation with my Gurg, saying I was sorry to leave and sorry for not being able to give him some food because our food was all packed and carried by the others. Gurg continued walking with us until he felt it was not safe for him to come lower. Shepherds were enemies of the wolves and everyone carried a gun. It was easy to kill an innocent animal.

We were delighted to reach an *aghail*, but when we went inside we saw that it was covered with deep snow. It was too late to look for another place, so we decided to spend another sleepless night there.

The accumulated snow in the *aghail* was more than a metre thick. We did not have shovels to clear the snow and even if we had, we could not clear enough. Besides that, we were dead tired, not sleeping for many days and nights because of the cold. With my eyes open, watching the stars, as it was a clear night, I thought of my American friend Jamshid. He must be in the US in a nice warm house with his family. The day before he left he phoned me and I could hear emotion in his voice, saying how sorry he was that his government had decided to pull US troops out. I told him it was not his fault. We had an enemy who used Islam as a weapon, penetrating the hearts and minds of our uneducated people. We failed to attract people despite defending them against evil, building schools, hospitals and roads for them, but they were only impressed by the preaching of the Taliban talking about heaven for those who fought us. A heaven full of food and drink, a heaven full of prostitutes. They did not even need to extend their hands to pick up fruit. All they had to do was wish it and the fruit would be in their mouth. For men who couldn't even afford to get married, the promise of prostitutes and food made them take up weapons against us and even blow themselves up among us, sending us to hell and themselves to a heaven where seventy-two prostitutes would be waiting.

I wanted the warm weather to come soon so we could start fighting the Taliban, the cheating, lying enemy. I would prefer that death to this slow death from the cold.

In the morning we started descending further, in spite of the danger of being seen by the Taliban, and were delighted to find an *aghail* with a roof. We were more surprised to find that inside this dry *aghail* was some wood to burn. We decided not to burn any wood during the day because the Taliban would see the smoke. Warming ourselves would only be possible during the night. Soon sleep came to all of us, but at least one person stood guard while others were sleeping, making sure to warn us if the Taliban appeared.

It was the best evening of our life in the mountain, sitting around the fire, watching our food warming up, smoking cigarettes, watching each other smiling, stretching our hands towards the fire. One officer from Parwan started singing and he had a very soothing voice. Then General Akmal Ameer, who was the best speaker and a poet, recited one of his poems:

Life is a stage for us to perform
Every individual sings his song on this stage and leaves
The stage is forever
I admire the song that people remember in their hearts and do not forget.

When we slept it was the deepest sleep of my life, once again one person walked around us the whole night guarding. Our blood was not frozen any more. Strength came back to us. Some soldiers competed against each other in arm wrestling. Jafar was a great storyteller and after dinner he told us stories – mainly tales he had heard from others – stories from *Shahnama, The Epics of the Kings*. We were delighted that this shelter gave us time for the warm weather to come. Then we could start our campaign fighting the Taliban.

But we were wrong to be so delighted. Eleven days later, our watchman informed us that a group of Taliban were walking towards the *aghail*. There was a debate as to whether to run away or to fight and finally General Akmal Ameer decided we would fight this group and after killing them we would climb to a higher place.

From where I was standing, I saw two Taliban crawling towards where we were, hoping they were not seen. But I had already spotted them. I was well hidden behind a massive rock, which made it impossible for the enemy to see me. One fighter was in front crawling and the other behind, following him. As soon as the man raised his head, my bullet reached his forehead. The man behind panicked and stood to run away, but my second bullet reached him on the head and he fell on his face. These killings made the enemy mad and they started advancing without cover shooting. Their foolishness gave us an opportunity to kill more than a dozen of them, but at the same time they managed to kill two of our companions. Believing they go straight to heaven fighting nonbelievers, they did not care for the cover. It was hard to know how many we killed because we had good cover and they found themselves obliged to attack to take our positions. But when they realised that their casualties were heavy, they started to shoot from behind rocks. I could not see what my friends were doing because I was shot at from all different directions. But at some point Officer Haroon came close to me and it was at that moment an idea came to me.

"Haroon, keep those guys behind the rock busy while I crawl to reach close, and then I'll throw two grenades."

"It is too risky Amir," he whispered back.

"We have no choice." And with those words I made my move. Haroon did not stop even for a second to let the Taliban see me.

When I reached behind their cover, I threw my first grenade and within a second the second one. Silence came from where they were. I looked back and saw Haroon standing with a smile. But at that moment, a bullet hit him on the chest. I realised each time we killed one Talib, at least five took his place, because they kept calling on their radios for more support.

Through the loudspeaker, the Taliban were shouting at us to surrender, telling us we would be forgiven. But we were not there to surrender. Firstly, because we all had one bullet to use against our own temples, and secondly, we did not trust the lying enemy. It was possible they would kill us anyway because we had already killed some of them.

There was more death among us. General Akmal Ameer was hit in the head and died instantly. Our comrades fell around us and even Basir Andarabi was injured. Taking Basir Andarabi on my back, three of us, Basir, Roheed and myself managed to break the enemy circle and ran away while the enemy continued firing. At times we had to drop Basir and respond to the fire. Basir, in that terrible situation, also fired until a bullet hit his chest and he was dead as well.

Now only Roheed and I had been left and we had no idea how to fight or escape. Fortunately, the darkness came to our aid but the Taliban had guns with night vision, which could see even in the dark. They used PARD NV007 A binoculars attached to their guns. These binoculars were easily available in Pakistan and Arab sheikhs provided the money for them, which cost less than $400. We knew the Taliban had plenty of money to buy the latest weapons, otherwise how they could fight the might of NATO?

"What we do, Roheed?" I said while continuing firing. "Not many bullets left."

"We are going to run towards them, there is no other way."

"But that is suicide."

"We have no choice, Amir."

As we ran towards the enemy, bullets passed our ears, hit near our feet but never hit the target. We ran and ran until no bullets came.

We ran for god knows how long until we found a cave and we both jumped in there, covering the entrance with a large boulder.

When I woke up it was late afternoon, according to my watch. We had slept for more than ten hours. Roheed was still fast asleep. We must have fainted because of exhaustion. My tongue was stuck to the roof of my mouth and I was extremely thirsty. After moving the large boulder, I stuck my head out of the cave. It had been snowing when we were fighting, but the snow was light. Now it was impossible to see more than 2m, which was good because the snow had covered our footsteps making it impossible for the Taliban to find us. But we could not leave that cave in case we headed directly towards the enemy. We needed visibility. So when Roheed woke up, we discussed the situation and decided to spend one more night there, hoping the snow would stop. Meanwhile we ate the fresh snow to quench our thirst.

Mullahs always made us scared of the darkness of the grave where we would be put at rest. Here the darkness had another dimension to it – the enemy with a gun. Through the small gap at the entrance to the cave, enough light came in for me to see where Roheed was, but the walls were black. What if snakes had a nest there and were spending the winter in a warmer place? What if the Taliban found us? They would keep shooting first to see if they could kill us that way. But if they saw us respond with bullets, they would blow up the cave. What if we ran out of ammunition?

In Islamic history, when Prophet Mohammad was attacked in Makkah, he and his close friend Abu Bakr ran away and took a refuge in a cave on a mountain. Once they were inside the cave, they worried about the enemy finding them. But spiders netted the entrance to the cave, giving the impression that no one had entered there recently.

We were both saddened by the loss of our friends and because of that were not in the mood for conversation. When night came, we could not sleep, and from time to time we checked to see if the snow had stopped. Fortunately, it stopped just before dawn, but we decided not to go anywhere until it was dark.

That turned out to be a good decision because once we left the cave to check if the enemy was around, we were shocked to see them like ants in large numbers going up and down the mountain, checking every corner.

We prayed that they would not come towards our cave because they would certainly suspect that someone was there, regardless of the boulder at the entrance. If we stayed there longer, more than another night, we were certain that the Taliban would discover us. We knew the Taliban would stop their search during the night, so that was the best time to leave. Around seven in the evening, everywhere was dark because of the cloud, but there was no snow. From where we were we could see the lights of Salang Tunnel, built by the Russians, severely damaged by the Taliban, which made it impossible to use. But it was renovated after the fall of the Taliban. This single tunnel had cut the journey to Mazar-e Sharif by six hours. We stayed put for another two hours, taking our military clothes off. We both had *piraan wa tonbaan* under our uniforms to protect us from the cold. At nine in the evening we ran fast towards the tunnel. We thought after half an hour we would reach it, but we were wrong. It took us almost two hours. Once we arrived at the edge of the tarmac, we panicked again because if we tried to stop a vehicle to take us to Kabul we might end up stopping a Taliban pickup. Taliban pickups looked like any other ordinary pickup used by civilians. At the beginning, hiding in the ditch near the edge of the road, we let the vehicles pass but also trained our eyes not to stop any pickup truck. But when we tried to stop cars, buses and lorries, none stopped. I had $300 on me, which I kept for an emergency. I would give all this money to a driver to take us to Kabul. In a normal situation the cost would have been only $10 for both of us.

☼ ☼ ☼

I don't know how much time passed but it seemed like eternity. We had escaped from a hell and could now be easily picked up by the Taliban while we were waiting for transport. God heard our prayers and a taxi stopped. It was on its way home.

"Can you take us to Kabul?" I asked, shivering.

"I was about to go home."

"We can give you good money." Roheed put his head near the open window.

"I am sorry, even if you give me good money, I have no time and I must get home."

"Listen, my good man, if you did not have time, you would have not stopped."

"Sorry, I was just curious and thought you needed help. No one at this time of the night is waiting for transportation. I thought one of you needed to go to hospital. I am a human being and don't want someone to die. Besides, the hospital is on my way to my house."

"Please sir, our close relative has died in the city and we must be in Kabul," I lied knowing the man had a soft heart.

"You know there has been fierce fighting around here and the Taliban are looking for some men. It is dangerous for me to take you and I think you belong to the group that fought the Taliban."

"Now that you know, we ask you kindly to help. I'll give you three hundred dollars."

"I like your honesty, guys. Let's pray nothing will happen. But you must get rid of those army boots." The driver pointed to our feet. "I'll go home to get you some shoes. Meanwhile I have a dirty tyre in my boot. Get your hands and faces dirty and wait in the roadside ditch exactly where you are. Keep hiding. I will find you."

We did what he asked us to do and went back to the ditch, but my heart was pounding. It was hard to trust anyone. The taxi driver who had brought our supplies to the mountain was the one who had betrayed us to the Taliban. He himself belonged to Taliban special forces, but we thought with money we could buy his loyalty. We did not know this taxi driver. But we had no choice.

Almost an hour later, the taxi driver stopped at the edge of the road, exactly where we were hiding. Roheed sat in the front seat next to the driver, and I sat behind him.

The driver stopped long before the checkpoints, asking us to walk parallel but away from the road, making sure that the Taliban at the checkpoints didn't see us. Sometimes we walked about 3km. By the time we reached Kabul, it was already daytime. Giving that $300 to the driver, we thanked him for putting his life in danger. The first thing we did was to go to a *hammam* for a wash. Roheed had $120 in his pocket to pay for the *hammam* and a very big breakfast.

A very big breakfast became two very big breakfasts for each of us. Now we were in a position to plan our future. Roheed and I started contacting friends who resided in Kabul to see if anyone was brave enough to give us shelter. But people were afraid of what was going to happen to them and did not respond when they realised the caller was one of us. Luckily one was either brave or crazy enough to help. By now the radio had announced what had happened to our group and the possibility of some of us being at large, warning citizens to keep away from us and if they spotted us they must report us to the Taliban police. We understood their fear. The Taliban were cruel and people worried about their own and their family's safety. But Najib, a friend of Roheed, was prepared to risk that. He had an empty apartment in Kabul and said we could go there for a while. Najib gave the address of the apartment to Roheed and told him to wait there until he arrived with the keys. Roheed told me he would go there alone first and when he was satisfied that the place was safe, he would phone me to join him. Clearly he was worried that the Taliban had made Najib offer help, just to capture us.

I stayed at the same restaurant drinking green tea, one after another. Having a proper meal and tea in a civilised place was a great novelty. Whose prayers helped only the two of us out of twenty-two to survive? And yet I knew that the danger was not over yet. Either things moved too slow in my country or I was too worried and impatient. Finally, Roheed phoned and gave me directions to the apartment. I immediately took a taxi and when Roheed opened the door of the apartment for me with a smile, I breathed deeply. He'd already prepared green tea for the two of us.

We found out that between 100 to 150 Taliban were killed, fighting us in Salang. They would do anything to capture and kill us. We did not go out. Najib brought food and drink for us. After several days in that apartment, we decided to emigrate to Iran. With the help of Najib we came up with an excellent idea. He would buy six sheep from Kabul, hire a pickup and both Roheed and I would act as sheep sellers going to Herat.

Before dawn, Najib came to wake us up. We met the driver with the sheep at the back of his truck. Pretending that we loved sheep, we both cuddled and hugged those sheep for a long time to get the smell of the sheep on our clothes. After that, Roheed sat at the front and I had the company of the sheep at the back. We sold the sheep for a quick and cheap price in Herat, a city that borders Iran. We would keep this money with the money we would earn in Iran to pay Najib back.

Chapter 17

Reasons for the Fall

By recognising the Taliban to be a legal opposition to the Afghan government, the US slowly paved the road for the them to appear in international politics and as they were now legitimate, they had the right to get weapons and support from any country they wanted.

The US was a contributor to the fall of the Afghan government. Ignoring a peace process that the government of Afghanistan planned, the US under President Donald Trump started negotiating directly with the Taliban and eventually signed a peace agreement with them, in which the Afghan government was not a partner.

I fought day and night, nonstop, in Farah province against an escalating and bloody Taliban offensive. Coming under frequent attack, we held the Taliban back and inflicted heavy casualties.

Not long after he came to power, President Joseph Biden said that American troops should not fight and die when Afghan forces were not willing to fight for themselves, ignoring the fact that we'd lost 66,000 army personnel.

It was true that the Afghan Army lost its will to fight. But that was because of the growing sense of abandonment by our American partners and the disrespect and disloyalty reflected in President Biden's tone and words. The Afghan Army was not without blame. It had its problems – cronyism, bureaucracy – but, ultimately, we stopped fighting because our partners already had.

It pained me to see President Biden and Western officials blaming the Afghan Army for collapsing without mentioning the underlying reasons it happened. Political divisions in Kabul and Washington strangled the army and limited our ability to do our jobs. Losing the combat logistical support that the United States had provided for years crippled us, as did a lack of clear guidance from US and Afghan leadership.

Two weeks before the government's collapse, while General Sadat was fighting in the city of Lashkar Gah, President Ashraf Ghani named General Sami Sadat commander of especial forces, the country's most elite fighters. He was called upon to come to Kabul. He reluctantly left his troops and arrived in Kabul on 15 August, ready to fight – unaware how bad the situation already was. Then Mr Ghani handed him the added task of ensuring the security of Kabul. But he never had a chance. The Taliban were closing in, and Mr Ghani fled the country.

There was an enormous sense of betrayal. Mr Ghani's hasty escape ended efforts to negotiate an interim agreement for a transition period with the Taliban that would have enabled us to hold the city and help manage evacuations. Instead, chaos ensued – resulting in the desperate scenes witnessed in Kabul.

So why did the Afghan military collapse? The answer is threefold.

First, former President Donald Trump's February 2020 peace deal with the Taliban in Doha doomed us. It put an expiration date on American interest in the region. Second, we lost contractor logistics and maintenance support critical to our combat operations. Third, the corruption endemic in Mr Ghani's government that flowed to senior military leadership and long crippled our forces on the ground irreparably hobbled us.

The Trump-Taliban agreement shaped circumstances for the current situation by essentially curtailing offensive combat operations for US and allied troops. The US air-support rules of engagement for Afghan security forces effectively changed overnight, and the Taliban were emboldened. They could sense victory and knew it was just a matter of waiting out the Americans. Before that deal, the Taliban had not won any significant battles against the Afghan Army. After the agreement? We were losing dozens of soldiers a day.

Still, we kept fighting. But then President Biden confirmed in April 2021 he would stick to Mr Trump's plan and set the terms for the US drawdown. That was when everything started to go downhill.

The Afghan forces were trained by Americans using the US military model based on highly technical special reconnaissance units, helicopters and airstrikes. We lost our superiority to the Taliban when our air support dried up and our ammunition ran out.

Contractors maintained our bombers and our attack and transport aircraft throughout the war. By July, most of the 17,000 support contractors had left. A technical issue now meant that aircraft – a Black Hawk helicopter, a C-130 transport, and a surveillance drone – would be grounded.

The contractors also took proprietary software and weapons systems with them. They physically removed our helicopter missile-defence system. Access to the software we relied on to track our vehicles, weapons and personnel also disappeared. Real-time intelligence on targets went out the window too.

The Taliban fought with snipers and improvised explosive devices while we lost aerial and laser-guided weapon capacity. And since we could not resupply bases without helicopter support, soldiers often lacked the necessary tools to fight. The Taliban overran many bases. In other places, entire units surrendered.

President Biden's full and accelerated withdrawal only exacerbated the situation. It ignored conditions on the ground. The Taliban had a firm end date from the Americans and feared no military reprisal for anything they did in the interim, sensing the lack of US will.

And so the Taliban kept ramping up. Our soldiers endured up to seven Taliban car bombings daily throughout July and the first week of August in Helmand province. Still, we stood our ground.

We cannot ignore the third factor, though, because there was only so much the Americans could do when it came to the well-documented corruption that rotted our government and military. That really is our national tragedy. So many of our leaders – including military – were installed for their personal ties, not for their credentials. These appointments had a devastating impact on the national army because leaders lacked the military experience to be effective or inspire the confidence and trust of the men being asked to risk their lives. Disruptions to food rations and fuel supplies – a result of skimming and corrupt contract allocations – destroyed the morale of my troops.

The final days of fighting were surreal. We engaged in intense firefights on the ground against the Taliban as US fighter jets circled overhead, effectively spectators. Our sense of abandonment and betrayal was equalled only by the frustration US pilots felt and relayed to us – being forced to witness the ground war, apparently unable to help us. Overwhelmed by Taliban fire, our soldiers would hear the planes and ask why they were not providing air support. Morale was devastated. Across Afghanistan, soldiers stopped fighting. We held Lashkar Gah in fierce battle, but as the rest of the country fell, we lacked the support to continue fighting, and retreated to base. Our corps, which had carried on in Helmand, was one of the last to give up its arms – only after the capital fell.

We were betrayed by politics and presidents.

This was not an Afghan war only. It was an international war, with many militaries involved. It would have been impossible for one army alone, ours, to take up the job and fight. This was a military defeat, but it emanated from political failure.

All apart from Ismael Khan were running away like mice from the mouths of cats. The chief of the army, President Ashraf Ghani, in his pyjamas and with slippers on his feet, sat in a helicopter with his American wife and millions of dollars he had stolen to go to another country. Many times he criticised the hero of the Afghan-Anglo war, King Amanullah Khan, for leaving the country after the mullah's uprising. But now this coward, without facing the Taliban, was on his way. At least Amanullah fought the mullahs until he was defeated and some months later tried again, fighting unsuccessfully. But Ghani was not that kind. He was a lying coward. He begged the United Arab Emirates to allow his helicopter to land on their soil.

The Taliban had not reached the Arg, the presidential palace, and the palace guard was ready to defend it, but after seeing the commander-in-chief fleeing, they lost hope, so they let the Taliban take the palace without a fight. The speed of victory surprised the Taliban because there was still a possibility they would be defeated by the guards.

The lion of Mazar-e Sharif, who challenged the US-backed government, was next, with the lion of Uzbeks Dostum and other important officials such as the head of security, the defence minister and the interior minister, all making their way to the United Arab Emirates by different means. Only Ismael Khan resisted the Taliban, until he was captured and shown by the Taliban on television in disgrace.

Commander Basir Andarabi, Commander Roheed, Commander Akmal Ameer and I decided with some other army officers to join the son of Ahmad Shah Masoud, Ahmad Masoud, who manged to keep Panjshir province under his control. He was the son of the famous Mujahideen commander and, frankly, I did not like the Mujahideen either. But between two evils, I opted for the lesser one. We took whatever weapons we had and stationed ourselves on top of the hills around Panjshir province waiting for the Taliban attack. Intoxicated by their victory, the Taliban used many ways to defeat us, such as invitations to join them. But we were adamant to defend Panjshir and, if successful, attack Kabul later.

To fight a powerful enemy one must have a leader who could command the resistance. Now we had no leader. Our generals fled the country immediately after the fall of the government. Some officers like me went to Panjshir to gather around Ahmad Masoud, although, as we had suspected when we met him previously, he was not like his father. He did not show clear leadership and was incapable of making the right decision.

The Taliban gathered almost all its forces and marched them towards Panjshir. They also received aerial support from Pakistan and Pakistan dropped its special forces personnel to fight alongside the Taliban. Nowhere else was left for the Taliban to fight, so almost all of them gathered on the road to Panjshir Valley. Capturing all army vehicles and weapons from the Americans after they left, now they were equipped with the best machinery in the world. Not only did we lack weapons, but we were also greatly outnumbered. Apart from officers, we had some dedicated soldiers with us and then we had the brave people of Panjshir. Men as old as 60 joined us to fight the Taliban, and boys as young as 14 also volunteered.

Unfortunately, Ahmad Masoud ignored me and my highly experienced commanders. Once again there was a failure in leadership. Disappointed, we left Panjshir but still trusted General Yasin Zia, who had escaped to Britain. He ordered General Akmal Ameer to go with us to Salang to fight the enemy. We accepted the leadership of General Akmal Ameer, a true hero who finally lost his life in Salang. The handsome general was only 35 years old. You know the rest of our fate.

We did not run away until the very last minute.

Appendix

Abbreviations

ANA	Afghan National Army
CIA	Central Intelligence Agency
DAGR	Defence Advanced GPS Receiver
GPS	Global Positioning System
HIMARS	High Mobility Artillery Rocket System
ID	Identification
IEDs	Improvised Explosive Devices
LAW	Light Anti-Armour Weapon
LRSR	Long Range Sniper Rifle
NATO	North Atlantic Treaty Organization
NGO	Non-Governmental Organisation
UAE	United Arab Emirates
UK	United Kingdom
UN	United Nations
UNHCR	United Nations High Commissioner for Refugees
UNICEF	United Nations Children's Fund
US	United States
USA	United States of America
USSR	Union of Soviet Social Republics
VHF	Very High Frequency